The British Citizenship Test

FOR

DUMMIES®

2ND EDITION

by Julian Knight

The British Citizenship Test For Dummies®, 2nd Edition

Published by
John Wiley & Sons, Ltd
The Atrium
Southern Gate
Chichester
West Sussex
PO19 8SQ
England

E-mail (for orders and customer service enquires): cs-books@wiley.co.uk

Visit our Home Page on www.wiley.com

Copyright © 2007 John Wiley & Sons, Ltd, Chichester, West Sussex, England

Published by John Wiley & Sons, Ltd, Chichester, West Sussex

Wiley also publishes its books in a variety of electronic formats. Some content that appears in print may not be available in electronic books.

ISBN: 978-0-470-72339-5

Printed and bound in Great Britain by Page Bros., Norwich

10 9 8 7 6 5 4 3 2 1

WILEY

About the Author

Julian Knight was born in 1972 in Chester. He was educated at the Chester Catholic High School and later Hull University, where he obtained a degree in History.

Julian was the BBC News personal finance and consumer affairs reporter for five years and has won many awards for his journalism. Previous to this, he worked for *Moneywise* magazine and wrote for the *Guardian* amongst many other publications. He has also authored *Wills, Probate, & Inheritance Tax For Dummies*, *Retiring Wealthy For Dummies*, and *Cricket For Dummies*.

Publisher's Acknowledgments

We're proud of this book; please send us your comments through our Dummies online registration form located at www.dummies.com/register/.

Some of the people who helped bring this book to market include the following:

Acquisitions, Editorial, and Media Development

Executive Project Editor: Daniel Mersey

Executive Editor: Jason Dunne

Development Editor: Rachael Chilvers

Proofreader: Anne O'Rorke

Cover Photo: Jack Sullivan / Alamy

Composition Services

Project Coordinator: Erin Smith

Layout and Graphics: Laura Pence

Proofreader: Jessica Kramer

Indexer: Claudia Bourbeau

Publishing and Editorial for Consumer Dummies

> **Diane Graves Steele,** Vice President and Publisher, Consumer Dummies
>
> **Joyce Pepple,** Acquisitions Director, Consumer Dummies
>
> **Kristin A. Cocks,** Product Development Director, Consumer Dummies
>
> **Michael Spring,** Vice President and Publisher, Travel
>
> **Kelly Regan,** Editorial Director, Travel

Publishing for Technology Dummies

> **Andy Cummings,** Vice President and Publisher, Dummies Technology/ General User

Composition Services

> **Gerry Fahey,** Vice President of Production Services
>
> **Debbie Stailey,** Director of Composition Services

Contents at a Glance

Table of Contents

Part III: Questions and Answers...................... 177

Chapter 9: Sample Questions and Answers for the Life in the UK Test 179

Answers 261

Index 275

Introduction

● ●

*B*eing British has been described as winning first prize in the lottery of life! And the 100,000 people who become British citizens each year couldn't agree more. This book is for you as a would-be citizen and welcome visitor to these shores.

Britain is a dynamic country, rich and diverse. It is a big hitter in the world, with a first-rate education system and cultural heritage to die for – although the less said about the weather and some of the cuisine, the better. No doubt, though, if you've picked up this book, you're already aware of a few of the benefits of coming to live and work in Britain, and ultimately of becoming a citizen.

Becoming a British citizen means enjoying full voting rights and access to all sorts of benefits, as well as the right to carry a British passport. See Chapter 6 for more on the rights and responsibilities of citizenship.

You'll find other books in the For Dummies series useful too; check out *British History For Dummies* (Wiley) as a useful research source for taking and passing the citizenship test.

About This Book

This book is about making your immigration and citizenship dreams a reality. In plain English, I take you through how to jump the administrative hurdles and cross that citizenship and immigration finishing line.

I outline all you need to know to get into the UK, stay in the UK – temporarily or permanently – and ultimately apply for British citizenship.

In a nutshell, here are the steps to citizenship I cover in this book:

- ✔ **Getting into and staying in the UK.** Initially you can enter the UK by obtaining a visa and a work permit. If you want to extend your stay, you have to fill out the right immigration forms in order to be granted *leave to remain* or *right of abode* (see Part I for more on what these mean).

- ✔ **Taking and passing the citizenship test.** After you've lived in the UK for long enough – usually five years – you can apply for citizenship. First you must take and pass the citizenship test (the Life in the UK test), or prove your English skills and knowledge of UK life by taking a course at a college of further education.

- ✔ **Attending the citizenship ceremony.** You take the oath of allegiance at the citizen ceremony. This is the proud moment when you officially become a British citizen.

Conventions Used in This Book

Immigration to the UK can be tricky, with lots of paperwork and fiendishly complex rules to understand, as well as a fair smattering of jargon.

Have no fears – the main aim of this book is to junk the jargon, and explain immigration and citizenship rules, and the paperwork, with crystal-clear clarity. I put new terms in *italics* and always follow them with an explanation. Web addresses appear in `monofont`.

As you look through this book you see text in grey boxes. The information in these sidebars is interesting (I hope) but not essential to your understanding of the subject matter. So when you see a sidebar, the choice is yours: you can read it, or not. No sweat if you decide to skip the sidebars – you won't be missing out on absolutely vital information.

Foolish Assumptions

In writing this book I make the assumption that you're not an expert in immigration, or in gaining citizenship.

I also assume you're willing to put in the hard work – you don't get something for nothing: you have to work at it! If you're going to reach your immigration and citizenship goals, you're going to have to show patience and take on the paperwork. The good news is that this book gives you the lowdown on all the paperwork you're going to come across, and points out relevant sources of help.

How This Book Is Organised

This book has three main parts. Each chapter in Part I looks at a different aspect of UK immigration from coming to the UK for a short stay to taking the citizenship test, all the way through to the rights you enjoy when you become a British citizen. Parts II and III include the revision material and sample questions and answers to help you sail through the test.

Part I: Becoming a British Citizen

This part covers getting into the UK by applying for a visa and the requirements you need to apply for citizenship. I give you an overview of all the players in the immigration and citizenship game and unravel the mysteries of the myriad forms and paperwork involved in immigration and citizenship.

Chapter 4 explains the preparation you need to do to take the test, and how to book and sit a test. If you pass the test – congratulations! – this part also describes the citizenship ceremony in which you celebrate your new status as a British citizen.

With all the paperwork and departments involved, it's no surprise that things can and do go wrong occasionally. Chapter 5 prepares you for potential problems with your application – forewarned is forearmed.

From a brand new British passport that enables you to travel freely in the European Union, through to free healthcare, and education, being a British citizen brings a wealth of benefits. Chapter 6 explains those benefits – and the responsibilities that come with them.

Chapter 7 is the fun part! This chapter lists ten useful *For Dummies* books that you may want to get hold of to help you integrate into life in the UK.

Part II: Revision Material

This part consists of the chapters from the Home Office's *Life in the United Kingdom: A Journey to Citizenship* on which the Life in the UK test is based. This part covers British history, festivals, and politics, as well as a fair few facts and figures about the population. You need to study this part carefully, because all the questions in the test are based on this information.

Part III: Questions and Answers

Part III contains over 300 sample questions so that you can start testing yourself in preparation for the Life in the UK test. I also include all the answers to the questions – no cheating, now! Study Part II, answer correctly the sample questions in Part III, and you'll be well equipped to pass the citizenship test with flying colours.

Icons Used in This Book

The small graphics in the margins of this book point to parts of that text that you may want to pay special attention to.

The information marked by this bull's eye highlights helpful strategies you'd be wise to follow.

Bear in mind the information this icon highlights to make crossing the citizenship finish line as simple as possible.

This icon highlights potential pitfalls on the road to British immigration and citizenship.

I sometimes go into a bit more detail about an issue raised in the text. You can skip these paragraphs if you don't want so much information.

Where to Go from Here

This book aims to help you navigate the UK's immigration and citizenship rules. You can read this book from cover to cover if you want to, or simply zero in on the information you need right now by using the table of contents and the index.

You may want to make notes as you go along – feel free to jot down comments in the margins of this book.

You may feel the need to use professional help in achieving your immigration or citizenship ambitions. No problem, head to Part I, which is dedicated to giving you all the points of contact you need.

Part I
Becoming a British Citizen

'Since moving to London we've seen a lot of the neighbours.'

In this part...

From applying for a visa and who you'll be dealing with in immigration, through to taking the citizenship test and celebrating your new status, this part has everything you need to know about becoming a British citizen.

Chapter 1

Deciding to Stay in the UK

- -

- -

*A*s a future British citizen, perhaps you've come to the United Kingdom to find work, study, marry, or even just to take in the sights. You like what you see and experience here – apart from the notorious British weather, no doubt!

Perhaps you lay down roots, master the language, and observe and appreciate the idiosyncrasies of British life such as queuing at any opportunity, and wearing socks with sandals.

The logical progression is to go the whole hog and apply for *British citizenship*, a qualification that enables you to play a full part in the social, political, and economic life of your new adopted home.

In this chapter, I take you through an overview of the journey from holidaymaker, visiting student, or worker to fully-fledged British citizen.

Plotting Your Path to Citizenship

Over 100,000 people become British citizens each year. Both the number of people coming from abroad to live in the UK, and applicants for British citizenship have risen sharply in recent years.

You can sum up the usual paths to citizenship as:

- ✔ Get into the UK through visas and work permits.

- ✔ Stay in the UK by being granted *leave to remain* or *right of abode* (see later in this chapter for more on these).

- ✔ Apply for citizenship by living in the UK for long enough and passing the citizenship test.

Looking at Why People Come to the UK

Your first taste of Britain, apart from films starring Hugh Grant and novels by Jane Austen, was probably by:

- ✔ **Coming here on a holiday.** Britain loves tourists and is proud of its unique history and heritage.

- ✔ **Coming here to work.** With a shortage of labour, Britain welcomes workers from abroad. The British economy is a star performer compared to many of its European rivals, with plenty of relatively well-paid jobs. Unsurprisingly, Britain attracts large numbers of people particularly from poorer Eastern Europe.

- ✔ **Coming here to study.** The UK is famed for its educational institutions. English is the world's premier language of business and the media, so it's no surprise that the UK is a magnet for foreign students.

Perhaps you came to the UK for more personal reasons such as marriage, or you're simply exercising your birthright to live in Britain.

The main reasons for people coming to Britain either for a short or permanent stay are

- ✔ Tourism
- ✔ Employment
- ✔ Education
- ✔ Marriage
- ✔ Birthright

Britain has a complex and multilayered immigration system in place to deal with every scenario.

Getting to Grips with the Visa System

When travelling to the UK, the first question you need to ask yourself – after 'Where have I packed my umbrella?' – is 'Do I need a visa for my visit?'

Do I need a visa?

A *visa* is a document that tells immigration officials at airports and seaports why you're coming to the UK and how long you're allowed to stay. The visa certificate is put in your passport or travel document by an immigration official at a British Embassy, Consulate, or High Commission in your country of origin. The visa gives you permission to enter the UK.

Not everyone needs a visa to visit Britain. People from some countries can come here on holiday without a visa but cannot study or work in the UK without one. Check with your local British Embassy, Consulate, or High Commission in your country of origin. You can find your local Embassy, Consulate, or High Commission at www. embassiesabroad.com. You can also take a look at the UK visa Web site at www.ukvisas.gov.uk for more details. You can apply for a visa via the post, in person, or online.

You can obtain a visa in your country of origin from a British Embassy, Consulate, or High Commission. You're charged a fee for the visa in the local currency. Chapter 3 has more details about the different types of visas you can apply for to stay or work in Britain.

If you require a visa to visit the UK on holiday or to visit family, the immigration official in the Embassy, Consulate or High Commission of your native country needs to see evidence that you intend to return. Take your return flight booking details as evidence that you intend to return to your native country.

Attending a visa interview

Your application for a UK visa may be approved by the immigration official in the Embassy, Consulate, or High Commission based purely on the application form. Sometimes, though, the immigration control asks you to attend a short interview.

The majority of these interviews are merely routine and are carried out in a public office at the Embassy, Consulate, or High Commission in your country of origin. However, you need a visa for the purposes of marriage – if you've married, or plan to marry, a British national – then the interview is carried out in a private room to respect your privacy during questioning.

The immigration official may want to ask you specific questions about your trip. For example, if you're studying, the immigration official may want to assess if you can support yourself while studying without recourse to working illegally (without a working visa).

An immigration official deals with your visa application. The chief immigration officer (CIO) supervises the immigration official. If you're unhappy with how the immigration official deals with your case, you can complain immediately to the CIO.

UK immigration rules allow for people to enter the UK to receive private medical treatment. You're required to provide evidence that you're coming to the UK for this reason. A hospital letter should suffice. Stays for medical treatment are usually limited to six months.

Working in the UK

The UK needs workers, both skilled and unskilled, to fuel its growing economy. The UK's immigration authority wants to ensure that those coming to the UK contribute to, rather than drain resources.

When deciding whether to allow you into the UK in the first place, or extend your stay temporarily or permanently, the immigration authorities make a judgement on your usefulness to Britain. Being highly skilled and educated, and already having a steady job or offer of work, are all factors that count in your favour.

Workers from the European Union

If you're from the European Economic Area (EEA) or European Union (EU), you're free to come to the UK and work. You can also bring your spouse and children along, who can also work or go to school, as long as they too are EEA/EU nationals. If your family members are not EEA/EU nationals, they'll need a visa and may not be able to work.

The citizens of 28 countries are defined as EEA/EU nationals. You can find the full list of countries on the Border and Immigration Agency (BIA) Web site at www.bia.homeoffice.gov.uk. EU countries include France, Germany, and Ireland as well as nations that joined in 2004 such as Poland, Hungary, Lithuania, and Estonia.

People from the new member states (that joined in 2004) must register with the Home Office before starting work. Getting registered is a formality. To obtain a Worker Registration Scheme application form (form EEA1), call 08705 210 224. The form EEA1 is very simple. You're asked for your name, address, date of birth, nationality, and employment details.

After you've worked legally in the UK for 12 months without a break, you have full rights of free movement and no longer need to register on the Worker Registration scheme.

Workers from outside the European Union

Work permits are issued by Work Permits UK, part of the Home Office's BIA scheme (Chapter 2 has more about the BIA). The BIA scheme enables UK employers to recruit people from outside the European Economic Area or European Union. Work permits also allow people from overseas to come to the UK for training or work experience.

Your would-be UK employer must apply for a UK work permit for you – you cannot apply yourself. Your potential employer needs to contact Work Permits UK at least eight weeks before the date you need to start work. Check out the government's Web site www.workingintheuk. gov.uk for more information about work permits.

The six types of work permit are

- ✔ **Business and commercial permits:** Enable UK firms to employ workers from abroad to fill vacancies that they can't fill with British citizens.

- ✔ **Internships:** Allow students from abroad to come to the UK on an *internship* (period of training) with an employer in the UK, usually as part of a course of study.

- ✔ **Training and work experience schemes:** Enable people from abroad to come to the UK to undertake work-based training for either a qualification, or simply work experience.

- ✔ **Sportspeople and entertainers:** Can come to the UK to ply their trade. You usually need a work permit but if you're coming to do personal appearances, you may come as a business visitor, in which case you don't need a permit. You also don't need a work permit if you have an invitation to perform at one or more specific events (such as concert venues or festivals). You may need a visa to enter the UK though.

✔ **Food-manufacturing industry schemes:** Allow people from abroad to come to the UK for up to 12 months to take up low-skilled work in the food manufacturing industry.

Although many work permit arrangements last a year or more, the idea is that you fulfil your contract of employment and then return to your country of origin.

If you come to the UK under work-permit rules your spouse and dependents can join you. However, your family has to apply for a visa at the local British Embassy, Consulate, or High Commission in their country of origin.

To find out more about issues such as whether you'll be taxed, if you're paid sick leave, or if you have the option to contribute to a pension scheme while you work in the UK, visit www.workingintheuk.org.uk.

Fast-tracking your way to a work permit

Special immigration rules relate to particular groups of workers such as au pairs, health service workers, and film workers. The idea is to allow easy entry into the UK for people with much-needed skills. For the inside track on how the rules affect particular groups of workers check out www.workingintheuk.gov.uk.

From 2008 the Home Office plans to introduce a new points-based system for people coming to the UK to work or study. The more points you have, the better your chances of being given the thumbs up to come to the UK. Check out Chapter 2 for more on the new points-based system.

Turning a Flying Visit into a Longer Stay

So you come to the UK, decide you love the old place, and can't bear to leave. You have two options when applying to stay for longer:

- ✔ You can return to your country of origin and submit an application from there.
- ✔ You can make your application to remain in the UK from Britain.

Perhaps the purpose of your visit is changing – for example, you initially visit the UK as a holidaymaker but then want to remain to study. You need to return to your country of origin and apply for a new visa through your local British Embassy, Consulate, or High Commission.

However, if you're looking to extend your stay in the UK for work purposes or to marry, then you can apply through the Home Office's Border and Immigration Agency (BIA)). Head to Chapter 2 for more on this big beast of the immigration jungle.

Marrying a Brit: No guarantee of citizenship

Sometimes people come to the UK and marry a British citizen in the belief that they themselves are going to become a citizen. I'm afraid it doesn't work like that. You don't automatically acquire British citizenship through marriage. You may be allowed *leave to remain* (this means you can live in the UK for a specific period, initially two years and then a further three years) in the country following a marriage – but marriage doesn't guarantee citizenship. You have to apply for British citizenship separately if you want it.

However, marriage can be a passport – excuse the pun – to *UK residency*, the right to remain in Britain. You and your spouse will probably be interviewed by immigration as part of the UK residency process. The immigration authorities want to be sure that the marriage is genuine – rather than contrived for the purposes of allowing the non-British partner to stay in the UK – before granting leave to remain.

If you're a British citizen marrying a national of a foreign country, you don't lose your nationality. In fact, you may eventually obtain *dual nationality*, which enables you to keep all the rights of a British citizen such as the right to vote in the UK, and also the rights of your spouse's country, providing that both countries allow dual nationality. If you gain British citizenship and your country of origin does not allow dual citizenship, it may consider you to have lost your original nationality, or simply not recognise your new British nationality – how rude!

Studying in the UK

To come to the UK to study, you must show the immigration official evidence that you've been accepted on a course of study at an educational establishment approved by the UK's Department for Education and Skills (DFES). Look at www.dfes.gov.uk/providerregister to find out if the college where you want to study is registered.

Overstaying your welcome

On expiration of your visa, you're expected to leave Britain in double-quick time. Even a delay of just a few days can cause a nasty scene with immigration and make returning to the UK difficult.

The sanctions taken against people who overstay in Britain can be severe. Overstaying on a visa is a criminal offence and can lead to detention, prosecution, a fine, or imprisonment. In addition, you're deported from the UK and are unlikely to ever be allowed back in.

In addition, you must be able to show that you can support yourself financially, without having to work.

When you finish your course of study and have graduated with a Bachelors or Masters degree you can stay in the UK for up to 12 months after your studies have finished and take up work. On completing their studies, other students must leave the UK.

You need to apply to study in the UK from your country of origin through your local British Embassy, Consulate, or High Commission. See www.embassiesabroad.com to find your local embassy.

Living in the UK: The right of abode

The *right of abode* is the right to live and work in the UK. When granted, it means you do not have to deal with the immigration services or obtain a visa, or a *right to remain* permit). The right of abode doesn't quite carry all the weight of citizenship – see Chapter 6 for more on citizenship rights – but it comes a very close second.

You have the right of abode if:

- ✔ You were adopted as a child in the UK by a British adopter.

- ✔ You're a citizen of a *commonwealth* country (former countries of the British Empire who are members of the Commonwealth organisation), before 31 December 1982, and one of your parents or adopters is a British citizen.

- ✔ You're female and became a commonwealth citizen before 31 December 1982, and are, or were, married to a man with the right of abode in the UK.

You can apply for a right of abode *certificate of entitlement* from the UK Home Office at: Home Office Nationality Group (Right of abode), PO Box 306, Liverpool, L2 7XS. You can also visit www.ukvisas.gov.uk. You have a gummed sticker placed in your passport, called a certificate of entitlement. The certificate shows immigration officials that you can move freely into and out of the UK.

Seeking Asylum

Each year thousands of people come to the UK from abroad – often smuggled into the country – and claim asylum.

In short, *claiming asylum* means that you ask to stay in the UK because returning to your country of origin is dangerous. Asylum claims are assessed by the UK immigration service and many are unsuccessful. As an asylum seeker, you're expected to return to your country of origin when it's safer. As a result, you're only initially granted a temporary leave to remain in the UK. However, eventually, you may be granted *indefinite leave to remain* in the UK.

Ultimately, a grant of indefinite leave to remain is on a case-by-case basis. Such a grant can follow marriage to a UK citizen, or after you've been in the UK for an unspecified period of time and show you're contributing positively to the life of the country, and putting down roots. Another factor that affects indefinite leave to remain is the situation of your country of origin; if you've fled a war zone, is it now safe for you to return?

Asylum seekers who satisfy all residency and citizenship test requirements (see Chapter 4) can apply for British citizenship.

If your asylum claim is turned down, you're expected to return to your country of origin. Common reasons for refusal to grant asylum include

- ✔ The immigration authorities believe that you would not be at risk if you return home.
- ✔ The authorities doubt whether you are who you say you are, or come from where you say you do.

Asylum seekers who are refused leave to remain can appeal against the decision. See Chapter 5 for more on troubleshooting immigration and citizenship applications.

Heading Towards Citizenship

People entering the UK today may not realise that in a few short years they can become British citizens, if they want to.

In order to apply for citizenship you need to meet certain requirements, including:

- ✔ You have to live in the UK with your British citizen spouse or civil partner for at least three years.

- ✔ If you're not married to a British citizen, you have to have lived in the UK for at least five years. You must not have been out of the UK for more than 450 days during that time.

- ✔ You have not been out of the UK for more than 90 days during the previous year.

- ✔ You must be aged 18 or older and of sound mind.

- ✔ You must not have been living in the UK in breach of the UK immigration rules at any time.

If you tick all the above, then congratulations – you can apply for British citizenship! The preceding requirements are just the start: you must also pay a fee, you must be competent in written and spoken English, and you must pass the British citizenship test. Chapter 4 has the inside track on how to obtain citizenship rights.

Gaining full British citizenship isn't simply about acquiring a natty certificate and then applying for a passport. British citizens enjoy freedoms and privileges that are the envy of many other countries. See Chapter 6 for the rights – and responsibilities – that British citizenship brings.

You can follow one of two paths to citizenship: *naturalisation* and *registration*.

- ✔ **Naturalisation** is when you come to the UK and fulfil the requirements to become a British citizen through the length of your stay and other factors, such as being married to your British partner for three years.

✔ **Registration**, a far less frequent route to citizenship than naturalisation, is open to citizens of Britain's overseas territories such as the Falkland Islands and Gibraltar. All you're doing through registration, is claiming your right to British citizenship.

Chapter 2

Getting to Know the Immigration and Citizenship Players

. . . .

In This Chapter

▶ Checking out immigration controls

▶ Meeting the main government agencies

▶ Making the most of charitable aid

▶ Resorting to legal help

. . . .

*B*efore you start your journey to British citizenship, you need to know about whom you're dealing with.

This chapter explains the roles of the different government agencies you encounter from when you first come to the UK to the time you gain citizenship. I explain how these agencies can affect your bid for immigration and citizenship.

Dealing with government agencies can be daunting but don't worry – this chapter also explains all the help and advice out there for you, from charities to legal help.

Understanding Immigration Controls

All countries look to control immigration. First up, immigration is about making sure that people coming from abroad to the UK have the right skills to add to Britain's social and economic life. Immigration controls also regulate how long people from abroad can stay; what you do when you're here; whether your relatives can join you in the UK; and whether you can use the National Health Service or claim benefits.

You can break down the immigration process into two different parts:

✔ Pre-entry clearance to come to the UK on holiday, for work, to study, or to marry, by obtaining a visa and/or a work permit.

✔ Permission after you're in the UK to remain temporarily or permanently through being granted *indefinite leave to remain* or British citizenship (see Chapter 1 for more about leave to remain).

The following sections explain the agencies involved in immigration and your goal of becoming a British citizen.

Meeting the Main Government Agencies

Say the word 'government' and many people think of faceless bureaucrats and professional paper pushers. Ditch the stereotype and bear in mind that the job of government agencies is to ensure that the law of the land is applied fairly. You have to work with, and cooperate with government agencies in order to make your British citizenship dream a reality.

British Missions overseas

People from certain countries need a visa to come to the UK, even for a holiday. Whether you need to apply for a visa or not depends on your country of origin and the purpose of your trip to the UK. For example, a holiday-maker from Australia does not need a visa, but an Aussie wanting to come to the UK to work for more than six months does need one.

You need to apply for a visa in your country of origin at your local British Embassy, Consulate, or High Commission. Your visa application is scrutinised by an immigration official – called an *entry clearance officer* or ECO – in the Embassy, Consulate, or Mission. You may be called for an interview to answer questions about what you plan to do while you're in the UK. Chapters 1 and 3 have loads more on who needs a visa and how to obtain one.

UK visas are often initially limited to six months. If you overstay your limit imposed by your visa without permission you can be prosecuted and deported.

Visa rules can be complex, so check out www.ukvisa. gov.uk for more details.

Work Permits UK

This agency does exactly what you'd expect, and deals with issuing work permits. If you want to come to the UK to work you may need a work permit to do so. See Chapter 1 for more on how to obtain a work permit.

Border and Immigration Agency (BIA)

If you want to turn your visit into a permanent stay you have to apply to the Border and Immigration Agency (BIA) in the UK for permission. This organisation is a branch of the Government's Home Office (the government department responsible for internal affairs). Put simply, the BIA's job is to decide who can and can't stay in the UK, whether for a couple of years to study, or on a permanent basis.

Sometimes you may see the BIA referred to as the Immigration and Nationality Directorate (IND). The IND morphed into the BIA in April 2007 after a re-organisation of the Home Office.

The BIA's job is to:

✔ Assess cases of people who are claiming asylum – removing those whose applications fail and integrating successful claimants.

✔ Decide if spouses or civil partners are to be allowed to stay in the UK.

✔ Ensure that people leave when they're no longer entitled to be in the UK, for example, when a visa expires.

✔ Decide if people can extend their stay in the UK.

✔ Assess and process applications for British citizenship.

As you can see, the BIA has a lot on its plate! The BIA employs thousands of staff. It can be bureaucratic and slow to make decisions. See Chapter 5 for more on average waiting times for applications.

Getting the Home Office fit for purpose

In 2006 the Home Office was hit by a series of major scandals about immigration. The most damaging headlines resulted from the failure to deport foreign nationals who, after arriving in the UK, committed crimes. The Home Secretary John Reid famously said that the Home Office was not 'fit for purpose'. In short, the system was swamped and rules disregarded . The Home Secretary's response was to break up the Home Office into two parts – one part responsible for immigration and prisons, the other the workings of the court (Ministry of Justice).

What does this mean for would-be immigrants? Well, the big idea of the shake-up is that immigration rules are followed to the letter and the whole system better able to do its job. Only time can tell if the reforms of the Home Office succeed.

The UK Foreign and Commonwealth Office runs the British Missions – such as Embassies, Consulates, and High Commissions – yet the Border and Immigration Agency is part of the UK Home Office. Why the difference? Simple: the British Missions deal with people based abroad, while the BIA works with people after they've come to the UK.

You can find out lots more about the BIA at their Web site at www.bia.homeoffice.gov.uk/.

The Immigration Service

This service is a subdivision of the Border and Immigration Agency (BIA) and deals with the screening and detention of asylum seekers. The Immigration Service also deals with immigration control at UK air- and seaports.

Feeling under the weather?

Britain is one of the few countries in the world to offer free universal healthcare. The National Health Service (NHS), one of the biggest employers in the Western world, treats millions of patients each year through a system of General Practitioners (GPs) and hospitals. Free NHS treatment is available for everyone living in the UK – not only British citizens. For more details, check out www.nhsdirect.nhs.uk.

If you're ill and need NHS treatment you must first visit a GP (unless it's an emergency, in which case you go straight to your local hospital's Accident and Emergency unit). The GP examines you and may refer you to a specialist doctor, called a consultant, for treatment. See Chapter 6 for more on the workings of the NHS.

Asylum and Immigration Tribunal

If the BIA rejects your request to remain in the UK, you may have the right to appeal against the decision. The Asylum and Immigration Tribunal (AIT) is your port of call. This organisation examines your case and decides if the UK immigration rules were applied properly in your case. AIT then decides whether you can stay or have to leave the UK. For more details on appealing an immigration or asylum decision, check out Chapter 5 or the AIT's Web site at www.ait.gov.uk.

Office of the Immigration Services Commissioner (OISC)

The Office of the Immigration Services Commissioner (OISC) exists to ensure that everyone receives the right immigration advice. OISC can't help with individual applications submitted to the BIA or offer advice, but they can point immigrants and would-be citizens in the right direction for help. The OISC Web site at www.oisc.gov.uk gives details about how to find an immigration adviser and how to lodge a complaint if you feel you've been badly treated by the BIA or other governmental body.

National Asylum Support Service (NASS)

As a new arrival to the UK, you're supposed to look after yourself financially so that you're not a drain on national resources by relying on the State to support you. However, if you're an asylum seeker, you're not allowed to work while your application to remain in the UK is being considered by the BIA. This leaves you in a catch-22 situation, particularly as you may have come to the UK with next to nothing. This is where the National Asylum Support Service steps in. Set up in 2000, the NASS allows asylum seekers access to health, education, and limited financial support – around £32 a week for a single person.

Casting an eye over the benefits system

The UK benefits and pensions system works on a *contributory principle*. This means that in order to claim Jobseekers Allowance or Incapacity Benefit for example – two of the main benefits paid to the unemployed and those unable to work – you have to have paid National Insurance Contributions (NICS). Logically, if you haven't been living in the UK then you haven't been contributing NICS, in which case you cannot receive certain benefits. For more on the UK benefits system check out the Web site of the Department of Work and Pensions at www.dwp.gov.uk.

In order for an asylum seeker to claim help from the NASS, you have to show that you're *destitute* (with no money or resources) or likely to become destitute in the next fortnight. Your local authority can help you find adequate nighttime accommodation as long as you apply for asylum 'as soon as reasonably practicable'. In short, this usually means within a few days of arriving in the UK.

Immigration Advisory Service (IAS)

Although funded by the Home Office, the Immigration Advisory Service has a history of independence and tends to be supportive of immigrants. The IAS offers free advice on all aspects of immigration and nationality law. In some instances they represent immigrants who have been denied permission to stay in the UK at appeal.

The IAS has offices at major air- and seaports as well as in large towns and cities. For more details on the IAS, and for online advice on immigration and nationality issues, check out their Web site at www.iasuk.org.

Nationality Checking Service

Immigration and citizenship applications involve a lot of paperwork (see Chapter 5 for the lowdown on all the form-filling). The forms can be complex, particularly if English isn't your first language. Therefore, many local councils offer a *checking service* that entails

- ✔ Looking over your application to ensure that you have filled it in correctly.

- ✔ Ensuring that you have submitted all relevant supporting documents.

> ✔ Seeing that you have the correct fee ready to send to the UK immigration authorities for your application.

This checking service isn't free; your local authority levies a small administration charge.

The BIA Web site contains a list of all local authorities offering a checking service. See `www.bia.homeoffice.gov.uk/`.

Calling on Charitable Aid

If you experience problems during your immigration process, you may feel as if you need more support than the agencies in the preceding section can offer you. Or perhaps you need advice that a government agency is not able to give you. Don't worry. Several charitable groups can offer help and advice with immigration and other issues relating to life in the UK.

Citizens Advice

You can find a Citizens Advice Bureau in most major UK towns and cities. These bureaux have advisers familiar with UK consumer and immigration law. Citizens Advice can advise you for free on the documentation you need to successfully apply for the right to remain in the UK, or to become a full British citizen. In addition, your adviser can talk you through what to do if the Immigration and Nationality Directorate refuses to let you live and work in the UK.

Take a look in your local *Yellow Pages* for details of your nearest Citizens Advice Bureau, or check out the organisation's Web site at `www.adviceguide.org.uk`.

UK Lesbian and Gay Immigration Group (UKLGIG)

The UK Lesbian and Gay Immigration Group is a support group for (you guessed it) lesbian and gay people with immigration problems. The group offers advice on form filling and challenging BIA decisions. The UKLGIG also campaigns against discrimination in immigration rules. You can call their helpline on 0207 620 6010, and visit their Web site at www.uklgig.org.uk.

Since 2005, all gay and lesbian couples that undergo a civil partnership ceremony in the UK have the same legal rights as married heterosexual couples.

Refugee Council

This Refugee Council offers advice and support to newly arrived refugees and people seeking asylum in the UK. Refugee Council workers focus on helping new arrivals obtain the benefits and accommodation you're entitled to as well as talking you through the immigration application process.

Here are the details for the Refugee Council:

- ✔ **England:** Call 0207 346 6777 or visit www.refugeecouncil.org.uk

- ✔ **Wales:** Call 029 2048 9800 or visit www.welshrefugeecouncil.org.uk

- ✔ **Scotland:** Call 0141 248 9799 or visit www.scottishrefugeecouncil.org.uk.

Getting Yourself Legal Help

I hope that you never have to use the information in this section, but things don't always go as planned. The organisations I list here can help you to deal with many aspects of the law.

Refugee Legal Centre (RLC)

The Refugee Legal Centre does what its name suggests. This charitable organisation focuses on refugees and asylum seekers who need legal representation. Perhaps you've been refused leave to remain and face possible deportation, or been turned down when you applied to bring over a loved one..

You have to make an appointment to see an RLC adviser by phoning their advice line on 0207 780 3220. Check out their Web site www.refugee-legal-centre.org.uk for more details.

Law Centres

Law Centres are dotted around the country. Law Centres are free to use and they usually have a worker who specialises in immigration.

Law Centres operate a strict catchment area policy. If you don't reside or work within the *catchment area* (the local area that the Law Centre covers) they may not see you – sorry!

To find out whether or not you live in the catchment area of a Law Centre, call the Law Centres' Federation helpline on 0207 387 8570. You can also visit www.lawcentres.org.uk.

What do points win? Entry rights to the UK

The UK immigration system has developed over many decades and is one of the most complex in the world. Some 80 different work and study routes lead into the UK – too many to go into here. From 2008 a points-based system for immigration is being introduced. Basically, you earn points according to several different factors such as your age, occupation, skills, and educational background. The points-based system is very similar to that already used by the Australian immigration authorities. You earn more points if you're young, skilled, and well educated. The more points you earn, the better your chances for getting the thumbs up to come into the UK.

Other lines of enquiry

Perhaps you find that the charities or Law Centres aren't much help to you, or maybe you aren't a refugee so can't ask the RLC for help. You can seek legal advice from a solicitor specialising in immigration law. Check out the Immigration Law Practitioners' Association Web site at www.ilpa.org.uk for details of local practitioners. Also worth a look is the Community Legal Services Web site at www.clsdirect.org.uk, which lists contact details of immigration specialists. Be warned, though, legal services don't come cheap and immigration cases and disputes have a nasty habit of dragging on and on.

If you're on a low income or have no income at all you may be able to claim legal aid to fund your immigration or asylum fight. Check out the Web site of the Legal Services Commission at www.legalservices.gov.uk for more details.

Chapter 3

Taking Care of Immigration and Citizenship Paperwork

In This Chapter

▶ Looking at visa forms

▶ Applying to extend your stay

▶ Dealing with immigration interviews

▶ Filling out the citizenship form

▶ Coughing up immigration and citizenship fees

*I*n this chapter I explain the forms you need to fill out and the supporting information and documentation you have to provide in order to achieve your immigration and citizenship ambitions. You can find these forms at the Web site of the Home Office's Border and Immigration Agency (BIA) at www.bia.homeoffice.gov.uk.

Deciphering Visa Forms

A visa, also called *entry clearance*, gives you the right to enter and stay for a specified period in the UK. For many people, getting a visa is the first step on the long road to British citizenship.

You have to apply for a visa in your country of origin at a British Embassy, Consulate, or High Commission (see www.embassiesabroad.com to find your nearest Embassy). The visa tells the British immigration officer at a UK sea- or airport your purpose of travel and how long you can stay in the UK.

The usual maximum period a visa is granted for a holidaymaker is six months, although you can try to extend this period (this chapter explains how). If you're a frequent visitor to the UK on business, for example, you can get a visa spanning one, two, or five years.

You can find several different types of visa application, which I describe below. They're just the main visa forms. You can also find forms for people such as diplomats, dependents of diplomats, and citizens of overseas British *dependencies* (countries that are effectively run by Britain). Take a look at the Web site www.ukvisas.gov.uk for more about these forms.

Non-settlement form (VAF1)

As the name suggests, the non-settlement form is the paperwork for people who want to come to the UK to visit, work, or study, but not to settle.

Settlement form (VAF2)

If you're the spouse, civil partner, or dependent of someone already living in the UK, and you want to come to the UK to live, you must fill in this form.

If you're the spouse, civil partner, or unmarried partner of a person looking to come to the UK to live, you're called the *sponsor*. As the sponsor, already living in the UK, you can help the application process along by providing documentary evidence that you can support the person planning to come to the UK financially and by providing accommodation.

Right of abode form (ROA)

The right of abode form applies if you're a foreign national who believes that, due to marriage or birth, you have the legal right to live – or *abode* – in the UK. (See Chapter 1 for more on the right of abode.)

Ensuring your visa application is correct

The Immigration Official at your local British Embassy, Consulate, or High Commission makes a decision on whether to issue you a visa based on the information contained in your application form.

Ensure that you complete the following information correctly on your visa form:

- ✔ **Your personal details.** Make sure that you enter your date of birth and nationality correctly!

- ✔ **The purpose of your visit.** You must be 100 per cent clear about why you want to visit Britain. If the immigration official suspects that your motives to travel are other than the reason you've given, they may refuse a visa.

✔ **The dates you want to travel.** The visa is valid for the specific dates you want to travel. You can ask for the visa to be *post-dated* (for travel after the time the visa is signed) for up to three months.

The immigration official often wants to interview visa applicants to double-check the information on your form and ensure that everything's shipshape. See the section 'Taking Immigration Interviews in Your Stride' later in this chapter for more on handling interviews.

Supplying supporting documents and information

Even if you swear on Scout's honour that you're simply coming to the UK to visit your mum, the immigration official may not take your word for it. You need documentary evidence to support your visa application. The documentary evidence you need to supply depends on what you say in your application. For example, if you want to study in the UK, you have to produce evidence that you can support yourself and that you won't work illegally. Documentary evidence may, for example, include statements of current savings accounts. Alternatively, if you're claiming the *right of abode* you need to produce your birth, marriage, or adoption certificate. (Chapter 1 covers right of abode.)

In addition to such case-specific information you need to produce your passport and travel documentation. The immigration official also needs a recent passport photograph (see Chapter 6 for more on passport pictures).

You have to pay a visa fee in your local currency to the embassy. Your nearest British Embassy, Consulate, or High Commission can tell you how much the fee is.

Applying for an Extension of Stay in the UK

In most instances a visa only allows you to visit or work in the UK for a relatively short time – usually six months. If you want to start laying down roots in the UK and ultimately make it your home, you have to have your stay extended for a specified period of time, or indefinitely

The two types of *leave to remain* (the right to live in the UK) in the UK are temporary or indefinite. If you're planning to simply work in the UK and then return to your country of origin, apply for temporary leave rather than indefinite.

As you can imagine, you have to fill in more forms to apply for an extension to your stay. Instead of your local Embassy, you deal with the Home Office's Border and Immigration Agency (BIA). (I discuss the BIA in Chapter 2.) You can find more information about the following forms at www.bia.homeoffice.gov.uk/applying/applicationforms/.

You need to apply for an extension of your stay *before* your current leave to remain expires. Allow at least six weeks to apply to extend your leave to remain, because the BIA often takes a couple of weeks to make a decision. If you return to your country of origin, then you have to apply through your local embassy for fresh permission to return to the UK.

Applying for a temporary extension

The following sections give you the lowdown on the forms you need to apply for a temporary extension to your stay in the UK.

Getting hitched in old Blighty

If you're a foreign national with limited leave to remain, you need to fill out the nattily titled *Form COA marriage or civil partnership certificate of approval* to obtain permission to marry or register a civil partnership in the UK. However, approval of this application does not give you leave to remain in the UK.

Form FLR (M)

This application form is for an extension of stay in the UK if you're the spouse or unmarried partner of a person permanently living in the UK.

Form FLR (O)

You need to fill in this form if you want to extend your stay in the UK and you're

- A visitor undergoing medical treatment.
- Working as an au pair, journalist, or language teacher.
- An employee of an overseas government or airline.
- A missionary.
- A writer, composer, or artist.
- A qualified nurse.
- A person with a British grandparent.

Form FLR (S)

You need this form to obtain leave to remain in the UK if you're a student or student nurse looking to re-sit an examination or write up an academic thesis.

Form FLR (IGS)

If you're a graduate, this form enables you to remain in the UK for 12 months after your studies have finished to find work. IGS stands for International Graduate Scheme.

Applying for indefinite leave to remain

Not surprisingly, *indefinite leave to remain* allows you to stay in the UK for as long as you want. This permit is a step up from obtaining your initial visa or extending your stay in the UK.

Surprise, surprise – you have the choice of a variety of forms to fill in.

Many local authorities in the UK offer an application checking service. Staff can look over your immigration application to ensure that you've filled it in correctly and that you've submitted all relevant supporting documents along with the fee to the UK immigration authorities. See Chapter 2 for more details.

You need to make any application to extend your leave in the UK or obtain indefinite leave to remain before your existing permission to stay in the UK runs out.

All applicants for indefinite leave to remain are expected to have taken and passed the British Citizenship test. Good for you that you have this book to show you how to pass the test with flying colours.

Form SET (O)

Put simply, this form is for the same groups of people who would fill out Form FLR (O) (see preceding section) with a couple of additions:

- ✔ Highly skilled migrants and work permit holders.

- ✔ Non-British citizens whose relationship in the UK has broken down due to domestic violence.

- ✔ People with long residence in the UK.

Form SET (F)

Form SET (F) is for your family members if you live permanently in the UK. Birth or adopted children under 18, parents, grandparents, or other dependent relatives need to complete this form.

Form SET (M)

This is the form for you if you want to apply for indefinite leave to remain in the UK as the spouse or unmarried partner of a person who's settled here.

Form BUS

No, it's not a double-decker . . . the BUS form covers both extension to stay in the UK and indefinite leave to remain for business people, private investors, and wealthy retired people.

Forms ELR and HPDL

Use these forms if you're an asylum seeker who was initially granted temporary leave to remain in the UK and you want to turn your stay into a permanent one.

Whether you fill in Form ELR or HPDL depends on when you first arrived in the UK.

Taking Immigration Interviews in Your Stride

At some point in your quest to enter and stay in the UK, or to gain British citizenship, you can expect to be interviewed by an immigration official at a British Embassy, Consulate, or High Commission in your country of origin, or by a UK immigration officer. Some interviews are simply routine procedure, and others are specific to your case.

Here are a few examples of immigration interviews:

- ✔ **Visa application stage.** It's standard practice for immigration officials to interview visa applicants.

- ✔ **On entry to the UK.** It's not uncommon for foreign nationals coming to the UK to be interviewed by immigration officials at the UK's air- or seaports.

- ✔ **Applicants for leave to remain.** You may be called for interview if you want indefinite leave to remain.

- ✔ **On claiming asylum.** If you claim asylum in the UK you can expect to be extensively interviewed by immigration officers. The officers need to fact-find so that they can reach a correct decision as to whether you'll be granted asylum.

Interviews can range from a few questions at passport control to a longer interview in private. Whatever the format of your interview, here's what you need to remember:

- ✔ **Always be truthful.** Obtaining a visa or leave to remain through deception is an offence under UK immigration laws.

✔ **Be polite and clear.** Immigration officers make decisions based on what you say at your interview, so how you present your case is important.

✔ **Consider legal representation.** If your case is complex, you may wish to consider having a lawyer who is knowledgeable about immigration law attend the interview. Refer to Chapter 2 for more on getting legal help.

When you arrive in the UK, make sure that you carry all your relevant documentation in your hand luggage in case an immigration officer wants to ask you questions.

Navigating the Citizenship Application Form

The two paths to citizenship are through naturalisation (another word for citizenship) and registration (both explained in Chapter 1). When you apply for British citizenship via naturalisation (the most common way), the main form you need is *AN Application for Naturalisation*. You also need to take and pass the British citizenship test or gain a qualification in English and citizenship from a UK college before filling out the form. See Chapter 4 for more.

Some of the things you're asked on the form are

✔ Your personal details such as your age and occupation.

✔ Details of any solicitor who is representing you in your application.

✔ The results of your Life in the UK test.

✔ Your parents' date and place of birth.

✔ Details of your marriage(s), present and past, as well as any children you have.

✔ All addresses you've lived at in the UK during the past five years.

✔ Precise dates for any time spent outside the UK during the past five years.

✔ Character references.

✔ Details of any criminal convictions.

The form is a hefty 16 pages long and takes a few hours to fill out properly.

If you and your spouse both want to apply for British citizenship you *both* need to complete your own separate *AN Application for Naturalisation* forms.

Paying the Fees

Dealing with immigration and citizenship paperwork is a bit like being a pelican – everywhere you look you see a bill!

From getting your hands on your visa all the way through to gaining British citizenship, almost every facet of the immigration and citizenship process involves paying a fee.

The following sections tell you the typical fees you can expect to pay.

Visa fees

- ✔ **VAF1 Non-settlement:** £63 for visitors, £99 for students, and £200 for work permits.

- ✔ **VAF2 Settlement:** £500.

- ✔ **VAF4 Right of abode:** £200.

You pay your visa fees in local currency in your country of origin.

Extending your leave to remain and indefinite leave to remain

- ✔ **Form COA for a marriage or civil partnership:** £135.

- ✔ **Forms FLR M, O, and SEGS:** £335.

- ✔ **Form FLR S:** £250.

- ✔ **Forms SET O, F, and BUS:** £335.

Citizenship fees

- ✔ **Individual naturalisation:** £268 (includes ceremony fee).

- ✔ **Joint naturalisation:** £336 (includes ceremony fee).

- ✔ **Registration of an adult for UK citizenship:** £188.

- ✔ **Registration of a child for UK citizenship:** £200.

- ✔ **British citizenship test fee:** £34

Fees are likely to rise over the next few years. The Government says that by 2008 it wants to use fees to generate income to help run the UK immigration service.

Chapter 4

Taking the Citizenship Test

• •

In This Chapter

▶ Understanding the basics of the test

▶ Making the right preparations

▶ Looking at what happens post-test

▶ Perfecting your English

▶ Attending the citizenship ceremony

• •

*T*ests have an image problem. Cast your mind back to school days and tests that invariably involved being stuck in stuffy classroom on a hot day, sitting in total silence for hours on end, being watched like a hawk by the teacher in case you try to cheat.

Fortunately, the citizenship test is not like going back to school. Sure, you need to study to take the test under exam conditions, but the whole process is a lot more, well, adult.

In this chapter, I explain what the test involves and how you can go about passing it with aplomb.

Delving into the History of the Citizenship Test

The citizenship test, or Life in the UK test, was introduced by the Government in 2005. United Kingdom residents seeking British citizenship are tested to show a sufficient knowledge of the English language, and of life in the UK.

The citizenship test is not designed to trip you up or weed out anyone who may not be contributing to British life. The test was introduced to ensure that, as a newcomer to Britain, you're adequately equipped for life here by encouraging you to familiarise yourself with the language, culture, and history of the British Isles.

The test makes gaining British citizenship really meaningful, and something to celebrate.

If you fail the citizenship test, you don't have to be pelted with rotten tomatoes and made to leave the country. You can stay in the UK and retake the citizenship test. See the section 'Retaking the Test' later in this chapter for more advice about it.

In 2007 the Home Office changed the rules about who has to take the test. Now, people who want the right to remain in the UK indefinitely have to take and pass the citizenship test. (See Chapter 1 for more on indefinite leave to remain.)

Preparing for the Citizenship Test

All the information that you're tested on in the Life in the UK the citizenship test is contained in the Government's study text *Life in the United Kingdom: A Journey to Citizenship*. You can buy the book from the Government's stationery office for £9.99. Check out www.tsoshop.co.uk for more details.

Or you can save your money: the crucial parts of this study text – the information you're tested on – is reproduced in Part II of this book. You can find plenty of revision questions to work on in Part III. Read and digest the information in Part II, get the questions right in Part III, and you should have no problem passing the citizenship test.

When you take the citizenship test, you're quizzed on some of the following topics:

- ✔ **Society:** The changing role of women, migration to the UK, and the attitudes of young people.

- ✔ **Culture and diversity:** The population make-up of the UK – its regional and ethnic diversity – as well as national traditions, and history of religious tolerance.

- ✔ **Government:** The roles of parliament, the judiciary, the police, and the devolved administrations in Scotland, Wales, and Northern Ireland.

- ✔ **Everyday needs:** How to buy or rent a house, where to access leisure and medical facilities, managing personal finances, and getting an education.

- ✔ **Employment:** Your rights at work, and full details on the UK's patchwork of sex and racial equality legislation. Very important stuff to know!

Going to College to Learn More

Further education colleges offer courses in British citizenship. These courses focus on the Government publication *Life in the United Kingdom: A Journey to Citizenship* study text, as well as telling you more about your new country. A number of colleges combine citizenship courses with English language courses. Look in the *Yellow Pages* or your local paper to find details of your closest college. The college of your choice can send you a *prospectus* – a brochure describing all the courses on offer.

You have to *either* pass the Life in the UK test *or* prove sufficient knowledge of the English language and British society by taking a combined English language and citizenship course before your application to become a British citizen is accepted.

Charities, voluntary bodies, and some churches and mosques have trained volunteers who can help immigrants. These volunteers may not have formal language teaching skills, but they can help new immigrants integrate and get to know more about British society. This knowledge all helps in passing the citizenship test!

Read all about it!

You can pick up a lot about British culture, history, politics, and attitudes through newspapers, both national and locally based. Reading newspapers can also help to improve your knowledge of the English language.

If you want to really get under the skin of Britain, and find out about its culture, why not swot up on its fascinating history? Lots of local colleges run courses on different aspects of British history. If you want an easy-to-understand overview, check out *British History For Dummies*.

Sitting the Test

Right – you've read Part II in this book, and tested yourself on the practice questions. You're ready to take the plunge and sit the test.

Around 100 Life in the UK test centres are dotted throughout Britain. Most major UK cities and towns have a test centre. To find your nearest test centre, call the Government's Life in the UK test helpline on 0800 015 4245. Alternatively you can visit the Life in the UK Web site at www.lifeintheuktest.gov.uk.

 Demand for citizenship tests is high – you need to book an allotted time with the test centre for you to sit the test.

Here are a few things to know about sitting the test:

- ✔ Forty-five minutes are allotted for the test.
- ✔ The test is carried out online at the test centre.
- ✔ You are asked a series of 24 multiple choice questions.
- ✔ The test fee is £34.

When you arrive at the test centre you're taken to a computer terminal to undertake the test.

If you're not very familiar with using a computer, fear not. The Life in the UK Web site has a specially designed guide to help you get to grips with computer basics such as operating a mouse. If you are visually impaired, software is in place to enable the computer to read the test questions out loud.

When attending the test you need photographic ID with you such as a passport or driving licence.

Passing the test

The pass mark for the citizenship test isn't hard and fast. The Home Office says it doesn't want to impose rigid standards. However, you're expected to get around 75 per cent of your answers correct. That equates to 18 right answers out of 24.

The test is marked online straightaway. If you pass, you're given a pass notification letter at the test centre. You need this letter when you're applying to the Border and Immigration Agency (BIA) for British citizenship (see Chapter 2 for more about the BIA).

If you sat a citizenship and English language combined test, you're given a certificate by the further education college (see the sections on learning English later in this chapter).

You now have to fill out *Form AN Application for Naturalisation*, which you can find at the Border and Immigration Agency (BIA) Web site www.bia.homeoffice.gov.uk. See Chapter 3 for more about this form.

Retaking the test

So what happens if you fail the test? Well, you're given the bad news in the test centre. Don't worry – you're not marched off to the airport and put on the first plane home.

In fact, nothing is further from the truth. You can carry on going to work, attending college, living with your partner, or looking after your family. The only thing that's changed is that you haven't met the criteria – yet – for British citizenship. No sweat, you can re-sit the exam, provided you're willing to pay the fee of £34 again. The next time – fingers crossed – with a bit of careful reading of *British Citizenship For Dummies*, you'll pass the test with flying colours.

If you do fail to pass the test again, try to assess why you didn't quite come up to scratch. Perhaps your weakness is the cultural questions, or the governmental questions in the test. Do some more revision on your weakest topics prior to retaking the test.

You can re-take the citizenship test any number of times. The only limit is how often you can pay out £34! However, you can't re-take the test within seven days of failing the test.

Pass the citizenship test first before applying for citizenship or indefinite leave to remain. The BIA expects to see a pass certificate with your application form, otherwise your form is disregarded.

If you lose your citizenship test pass certificate you won't be issued with a new one – you have to go through the whole thing again! So keep it safe.

Talking About the English Language Requirement

Passing the citizenship test is enough to meet the other requirement for British citizenship, which is to display competence in the English language. However, the other route is to take the citizenship qualification combined with an English language qualification.

In order to be granted citizenship you also need to have lived in the UK for a specific period of time and not to have been in breach of the UK immigration rules at any time. Check out Chapter 1 for more on citizenship requirements.

If you are over 65 or have a mental impairment then it may be possible for you to bypass the citizenship test or citizenship/language requirements and still qualify as a British citizen. The Home Office has discretion over whether to grant citizenship without evidence of your ability to speak English, and without you having passed the Life in the UK test.

Proving competence in English

If your English skills aren't at a sufficient level to pass the citizenship test, in order to prove that you're competent at English you must attain the qualification *English for Speakers of Other Languages (ESOL) Entry Three*.

Put simply, ESOL Entry Three demonstrates that you have the ability to hold a conversation on a straightforward topic, such as the weather (a pre-occupation amongst the British), or a trip to the shops. You don't have to be word perfect in your conversation, or use exactly the right grammar. To attain ESOL Entry Three, you simply have to get your point across in an understandable way.

Taking an ESOL course

ESOL is taught at colleges. Have a look at the 'Education and learning' section on the Government's public services Web site at www.direct.gov.uk. You can search for a course on this Web site.

Alternatively, to find out more about ESOL and citizenship classes, contact your local college direct (you can find the details in *Yellow Pages*), or call the Government's Life in the UK test helpline on 0800 015 4245.

Course fees depend on the college you choose to study at, but some offer to register you on an ESOL level 1 course for as little as £10. You can build up through ESOL levels 1, 2, and 3 or you can go straight for level 3. Assessment is by a paper-based test and you are free to ask to be tested at any time. Some courses last a couple of months, with one session a week, while others last six months or a little longer. The rule of thumb is that the longer the course, the more in-depth the citizenship study.

You can have your English assessed at a Learn Direct centre. Learn Direct is an organisation that aims to boost education and skills amongst adults. Learn Direct operates a network of more than 2,000 online learning centres in the UK. They operate a helpline on 0800 101 901, and Web site at www.leanrdirect.co.uk.

Chatting in Gaelic or Welsh

Britain is made up of distinct countries: England, Scotland, and Wales, as well as Northern Ireland. English is, by a long way, the main language spoken in the UK. However, Scotland and Wales both have their own national languages – Scots Gaelic and Welsh. If you can prove competence in either of these two languages then you can pass the language skills part of the citizenship test. In other words, you don't have to be fluent in English if you can speak Scots Gaelic or Welsh.

However, both Scots Gaelic and Welsh are minor languages, spoken by relatively small numbers of people in the UK. If you want to really integrate in British society, you're best advised to get your English up to scratch.

Celebrating with a Citizenship Ceremony

The British citizenship ceremony has proved a big hit. After all, everyone loves a celebration and that's exactly what the ceremony is.

The ceremony marks the happy event of moving to citizenship and the granting of full voting and other rights. See Chapter 6 for more on what rights citizenship brings.

Attending the ceremony

Citizenship ceremonies are held in town halls and registry offices throughout the country, organised by local authorities. New citizens are invited and can bring along family, friends, and well-wishers. Usually between 12 and 24 new citizens attend each ceremony. The local authority may limit the number of guests you can invite to your ceremony, so check with the organising authority before inviting all your relatives!

Superintendent registrars preside over the ceremony – the same people who conduct civil weddings. As a new citizen, you take an oath of allegiance (see the next section). To add a little more gravitas to the occasion, sometimes local dignitaries, such as the mayor, may attend the ceremony, and the national anthem may be played.

Citizenship ceremonies are compulsory (as if you needed an excuse to party!). After you receive your letter from the Border and Immigration Agency (BIA) telling you that you're being granted British citizenship, you have 90 days to attend a ceremony. (The BIA can take several months to process your application for citizenship.) Your local authority contacts you with a date for your ceremony.

Sleeping in and missing your ceremony can be a costly error. If you don't attend a ceremony within 90 days of being told to, you have to go through the whole citizenship application process again, and pay all the fees again. However, you don't have to re-sit the citizenship test, or the citizenship and English language course.

Throwing a private party

Some local authorities give you, as a new citizen, the option of your own private ceremony with just friends and family, presided over by the registrar. However, privacy comes at a cost. Expect to pay around £100 for a private citizenship ceremony.

The cost of your citizenship ceremony is included in your nationality application fee, currently £268 for an individual (see Chapter 3 for the full list of fees).

Taking the oath of allegiance

At the centre of the citizenship ceremony is the moment when you take the oath of allegiance. Here's the oath:

> I (*your name*) swear by Almighty God that, on becoming a British citizen, I will be faithful and bear true allegiance to Her Majesty Queen Elizabeth the Second, Her Heirs and Successors according to law.

> I will give my loyalty to the United Kingdom and respect its rights and freedoms. I will uphold its democratic values. I will observe its laws faithfully and fulfil my duties and obligations as a British citizen.

As you can see, the oath is designed to remind you of the responsibilities of British citizenship.

A religious reference to 'Almighty God' is included in the oath, but this is a very generic reference and can be taken by people from a Christian and non-Christian background. No alternative form of words is offered for atheists.

You won't need to memorise the oath! Generally, the presiding officer reads out the oath and you and the other new citizens simply repeat it.

After you take the oath, you're handed your citizenship certificates. Your certificate is both a keepsake and a handy document, because you can use it to get your first British passport (read Chapter 6 for information about getting your passport).

The oath of allegiance is extremely important. It signifies the moment when you become a British citizen.

Chapter 5

Troubleshooting Your Application

. . . .

In This Chapter

▶ Looking at what can go wrong

▶ Examining your rights to appeal against decisions

▶ Being aware of the waiting times involved

▶ Coping with citizenship rejection

▶ Knowing about deportation

. . . .

*H*opefully your path to citizenship will be straightforward. But you have to deal with a lot of bureaucracy and you may be unfortunate enough to encounter instances where you fall foul of immigration rules or simply find yourself at the mercy of an unsympathetic official. To keep your immigration status and your ultimate British citizenship ambitions on track, you need to know how to troubleshoot.

In this chapter, I explain what can go wrong with your immigration and citizenship bid, and how to go about appealing decisions.

Being Aware of What Can Go Wrong

Chapter 1 of this book gives you a good idea of just how complex UK immigration law is. Unfortunately, just to confuse and frustrate matters further, you have to throw human error into the mix. Now, I don't want to scare you off, but I do want to make you aware of potential mishaps.

Here are some of the problems you may encounter with your immigration and citizenship bid:

- ✔ **People can lose vitals forms.** Protect yourself from the authorities losing your paperwork by obtaining duplicates of all your vital documents, such as your birth certificate, and keeping them safe.

- ✔ **Immigration interviews can go wrong.** At certain stages of the immigration process (such as when you first apply for a visa to come to the UK, or following your marriage to a British citizen), you may be asked to attend an interview. The interview is with an immigration official. Immigration interviews aren't meant to be a witch-hunt but sometimes, due to poorly trained staff, or the simple fact that the official is in a bad mood, you can find they can take a nosedive. In the worst-case scenario, the official can accuse you of lying about your application.

The Government-funded Immigration Advisory Service recommends that you register an immediate complaint if you feel you haven't received a fair hearing at a visa interview. Ask to speak to the chief immigration officer – the immigration official's boss – and tell him or her of your concerns.

✔ **Officials can make wrong judgement calls.**
Immigration law is very complicated and sometimes officials can interpret the law wrongly. According to the IAS, one of the most common errors is when an official tells you that you've no right of appeal against a decision. The answer is to seek a second opinion as to whether you can appeal. Check out Chapter 2 for details of charities and other bodies that can help.

The Asylum and Immigration Tribunal handles appeals against immigration decisions. You can find out more about them by visiting www.ait.gov.uk or calling 0845 6000 877.

Understanding Your Right of Appeal

You can appeal against certain immigration decisions but not others.

Decisions you can appeal against include the following:

✔ Refusal of entry to the UK when you arrive at a UK air- or seaport.

✔ Refusal to allow you to vary or extend your leave to stay in the UK.

✔ Refusal to allow you to visit the UK when you plan to visit a family member during your stay. A family member is defined as first cousin or closer.

✔ A decision to have you deported.

The decisions you have no right of appeal against include:

- ✔ Refusal of a visa when you want to come to the UK but are not visiting a family member.

- ✔ You're a student planning to come to the UK to study on a course lasting less than six months.

- ✔ Refusal of a work permit. However, you and your potential employer are free to submit new supporting evidence for the immigration authorities to reconsider your case.

If you want to extend your leave to remain in the UK, you have to apply to do so before your visa expires.

Appealing against an immigration decision

The appeals process can be long and laborious and complex cases can take many months to sort out. You can represent yourself at the appeal hearing but in serious cases you may need legal representation, especially for cases of immigration dispute such as denial of leave to remain. (Look at Chapter 2 for details of legal help you can call upon.)

The time limit for lodging an appeal varies:

- ✔ In cases of an overseas refusal – in other words you're denied entry into the UK from your country of origin – you have 28 calendar days in which to lodge an appeal.

> ✔ With a refusal in the UK you have just 12 working days (not including weekends and Bank Holidays) to lodge an appeal.

> ✔ If you're in detention (you're in custody awaiting deportation) the time limit for appeals is just five working days (not including weekends and Bank Holidays).

You can download appeal forms at the AIT Web site at `www.ait.gov.uk/forms_and_guidance/forms_and_ guidance.htm`. You return the forms to the AIT.

You're notified in writing of the date, time, and place of your appeal hearing, and you're sent directions to the hearing centre where your appeal is to be heard. If you live outside the UK, the hearing takes place in your absence.

If you're late lodging an appeal you may lose your right to appeal.

Legally qualified immigration judge(s) hear appeals. You can have legal representation and can call witnesses. At the hearing, a Home Office representative explains why your immigration application has been turned down. The judge examines the evidence, both written and oral, and may ask you questions. The judge ultimately comes to a decision called a *determination*, which is sent to you in writing within 10 days.

Appeals against the denial of an asylum are fast-tracked. Sometimes appeals don't go to a full appeal hearing. Initially appeals are assessed at a 30-minute case management review (CMR) hearing presided over by a judge who has the power to assess an appeal without going to a full hearing.

Finding the right appeal form

You have three main appeal forms to choose from. The forms can all be downloaded from the Asylum and Immigration Tribunal Web site at www.ait.gov. uk. Look on the Web site for guidance on filling out each form.

Here's a brief run-down of each appeal form:

✓ **Form AIT1:** Use this form if you want to appeal against a decision made in the UK when you're also in the UK.

✓ **Form AIT2:** Fill out this form to appeal against a decision made by a visa officer abroad. You use this form in your country of origin.

✓ **Form AIT3:** You need this form if you want to appeal against an immigration decision made inside the UK after you've left the UK.

You can find further details on how to make a complaint in the 'contact us' section at the Web sites www.ukvisas. gov.uk or www.bia.homeoffice.gov.uk.

Playing the Waiting Game

When it comes for dealing with immigration and citizen-ship, sadly you can't wave a magic wand and get instant results. The following sections give you an idea of the waiting times involved.

Hanging on for an immigration decision

Anyone dealing with the UK immigration service can tell you that it's the time officials spend making decisions, rather than administrative errors, that piles on the frustration.

Waiting times for a decision vary according to the individual case and the type of application you're making. Generally, visa decisions are made quickly – in a matter of weeks or even days.

In more complex cases, such as extending leave to remain, decisions about visas can take weeks or even months. Asylum seekers can wait many months for a decision on getting leave to remain.

The BIA Web site gives some broad guidance on how long you can expect to wait for each immigration scenario. Look at www.bia.homeoffice.gov.uk/applying.

The IAS advises that if you appeal against an immigration decision, you can expect to wait several months for your case to be heard. Asylum *appeals*, however, are now being fast-tracked. A full appeal hearing can take place within four weeks of the appeal being lodged.

You're told in writing when your appeal hearing is being held, so be as patient as you can!

Holding out for a citizenship decision

When you pass the citizenship test (Life in the UK test) you're given a confirmation letter at the test centre. If you choose the combined English language and citizenship course route, your college supplies you with a certificate. You then send off the confirmation letter or certificate with your application for citizenship to the Border and Immigration Agency (BIA) – see Chapter 3 for the ins and outs of this process.

According to the BIA you can expect your citizenship application to be checked and processed in around five months.

If you want to check progress on your application or have any questions relating to it, you can call the BIA's call centre on 0845 010 5200.

All being well, you're told in a letter from the BIA that your application has been accepted. You're then in the home stretch. The final thing you have to do is attend a citizenship ceremony and become a true blue British citizen – congratulations!

Dealing with a Citizenship Rejection

The BIA rejects around one in seven applications for British citizenship. The main reason for rejection is if the applicant hasn't lived in the UK for long enough (five years, or three years with a British partner) or has spent a long period of time (450 days) out of the UK during the previous five years.

If you're one of the unlucky ones who is rejected, the BIA should explain the reason for your rejection. If you need further clarification, call their call centre on 0845 010 5200.

If you're rejected for British citizenship the first time around, the good news is that you can reapply at a later date.

You may want to use the Nationality Checking Service before submitting any forms to the BIA. Many local councils offer a checking service that looks over your application and supporting documents to ensure that everything's in order. See Chapter 2 for more on the checking service.

Thinking the Unthinkable: Deportation

Under certain circumstances (such as if you've committed a crime while in the UK), the courts can decide that, as a foreign national, you are to be deported from the UK and returned to your country of origin. However, ultimately the Home Secretary, as head of the immigration service, decides whether or not to carry out the court's orders. Alternatively, the move to have you deported can come from the Immigration Service if, for example, you've been found to have overstayed on a visa or to have broken the terms of your stay in the UK.

Deportation is relatively rare when compared to the numbers of people departing voluntarily, or the 100,000 plus people each year who obtain British citizenship and make the most of life in their new home.

Grounds for deportation include the following situations:

- ✔ You're convicted of a criminal offence in the UK and the trial judge has recommended deportation.

- ✔ You've overstayed your visa.

- ✔ Your claim for asylum has been rejected and you've not left the UK voluntarily.

The Home Office informs you in writing that you're going to be removed from the UK.

A detention order is often issued at the same time as a deportation notice. Put simply, a _detention order_ means that you're taken into custody, where you remain under lock and key until the time comes for you to be deported.

It's possible for you to appeal against deportation. If you find yourself in this position, you need legal help, fast. Chapter 2 explains how to obtain appropriate legal representation.

A British citizen or someone with the _right of abode_ (see Chapter 1 for more about this right) cannot be deported.

Chapter 6

Reaping the Rewards of Citizenship

*B*ritish citizenship is a passport – pardon the pun – to an array of rights and privileges. British citizens enjoy freedoms and perks that are the envy of many other countries.

In addition, by choosing Britain as your home, you have the benefit of lots of rights such as free medical treatment and education.

In this chapter, you can examine your rights as a citizen and resident.

Unlike many other countries, such as the United States, Britain doesn't have a Bill of Rights. No single document sets out an individual's rights and what the Government or judiciary can and can't do. Instead, British citizens enjoy a patchwork of protection through many centuries of parliamentary legislation and legal rulings. In addition, Britain does subscribe to the Convention on Human Rights – see the later section 'Examining the Human Rights Act'.

Taking Part in the Democratic Process

Being a British citizen gives you the right to vote in general, local government, and European parliamentary elections – provided you're over the age of 18, are not imprisoned for a criminal offence, and do not have a severe mental health problem.

In order to be able to vote, your name has to appear on the *electoral register*, the list of people who live in a *constituency* (local area) who are eligible to vote.

It's quite simple to get your name on the electoral register. Every year local councils send out forms to all households in their areas asking for details of everyone living in the house who is eligible to vote. You can wait for one of these forms to land on your doormat, or alternatively you can give your local council a call and ask them to send you a form through the post. You can find the number of your local council in the *Yellow Pages*.

If you don't fill in and return your electoral register form, you can be prosecuted and fined.

You have the right to vote but that doesn't mean that you have to exercise it.

A whirlwind tour of Parliament

The British parliament consists of an elected House of Commons and the appointed House of Lords. Members of the House of Lords are appointed by the Queen but on the say-so of the Government. The Government – including the Prime Minister – is drawn from the biggest political party or coalition of parties in the Commons.

As far as law-making is concerned, the House of Commons is far more important than the Lords. The House of Lords can't overturn legislation passed by the Commons; all it can do is delay the law coming into force for a few months. The upshot of this power merry-go-round is that real political clout is concentrated in the hands of the Prime Minister and Cabinet.

Britain is the world's oldest parliamentary democracy – over 700 years old in fact. Yet in the distant past only men who owned land had the right to vote. During the 19th century, the right to vote was extended to more and more people, and finally, in 1918, women were given voting rights.

British History For Dummies gives a fascinating overview of political history if you want to find out more.

Perhaps, as a British citizen, you decide to live in another European Union country. In that case you can vote in that country's elections (provided you have registered) or alternatively, you can choose to continue to vote in British elections.

Examining the Human Rights Act

The Convention on Human Rights is the closest thing Britain has to a Bill of Rights and yet it isn't even British! The Convention was drawn up by the European Union and its provisions were enacted into British law in 1998, through the Human Rights Act. As the name suggests, the Convention guarantees certain basic human rights.

Don't think that prior to the convention being adopted into British law, UK society ignored such things as the right to life or liberty. In fact, in most cases, all the convention does is to formalise rights that already existed due to centuries of domestic law-making and legal precedent.

As a British citizen, you have

- The right to life, and not to be condemned to death or execution.
- The right not to be tortured or treated in an inhumane or degrading way.
- The right to liberty and security.
- The right to a fair trial and not to be punished without due legal process.
- The right to respect for your private and family life.
- The right to marry and have a family.
- Freedom from discrimination.
- Freedom of religion, conscience, and thought.
- Freedom of speech.
- The right of peaceful assembly and demonstration.
- The right to protect your property.
- The right to an education.

That's a lot of rights!

The Human Rights Act grants *absolute* and *qualified* rights. As a British citizen, you have an absolute right to life, which means you may not be killed for *any* reason, even if you commit a heinous crime. *Qualified rights* try to strike a balance between your rights and the rights of everyone else. For example, you have the right to freedom of speech, but not if you use that freedom to incite discrimination.

Looking Beyond the Human Rights Act

The provisions of the Human Rights Act contain only a fraction of your rights as a British citizen. A whole plethora of laws grant you extra rights.

You have

- The right to have your personal data protected
- The right to information
- The right to medical treatment
- The right to an education
- The right to work
- The right to a home

The following sections explain these rights in more detail.

The right to have your personal data protected

The 1998 Data Protection Act states that data held about you by government agencies and businesses has to be accurate, secure, and up to date.

What's more, only relevant people should be given your personal data. Therefore, for example, your bank shouldn't be able to access your medical records.

Personal data includes information such as your medical records, credit reference files, and employment record.

The right to information

The 2000 Freedom of Information Act is relatively new but it provides a big expansion to the rights of the British citizen. Put simply, this law gives you the right to ask for previously private information from public bodies such as local councils or the Government. For example, you may want to find out how much your council is spending on installing speed bumps in your road, or what your local health authority is forking out on paper clips. Any British citizen is free to put in a Freedom of Information request and expect to have it answered.

When making a request under the Freedom of Information Act, put it in writing. The public body must have a good reason to refuse to supply you with the information you request.

For more details on how the Act works, check out the Office of the Information Commissioner's Web site at www.informationcommissioner.gov.uk.

The Freedom of Information Act only applies to public bodies; not to businesses, or individuals.

The right to medical treatment

The British National Health Service (NHS) has its critics but nevertheless it offers free healthcare, delivered at the point of need. You have the right to apply to be registered with a NHS doctor – called a *general practitioner* or GP for short. The GP has the right to refuse to add you to his or her list, but you have thousands of GPs to choose from, so finding a local GP to register with won't be a problem.

GP's are the gatekeepers of the NHS. It's up to them to refer you to a hospital for treatment – unless it's an emergency, in which case you go to the accident and emergency department of your local hospital.

The right to medical treatment doesn't only apply to British citizens. Even if you're simply visiting from abroad, you're entitled to treatment if, say, you have an accident. The UK also provides an extensive private health service that you can use, as long as you're prepared to pay.

The right to an education

Any child living in Britain is entitled to free state education. But with rights come responsibilities – as a parent you're legally obliged to ensure that your children attend a school between the ages of 5 and 16. You don't have to send your children to a state school; you're free to send your child to a private school or even have him or her tutored at home.

The right to work

All British citizens can work without restrictions. Laws guarantee that workers – whether British or from abroad – receive a minimum wage.

Under the minimum wage law, workers over the age of 18 are guaranteed an hourly wage of least £5.35 from October 2006. Younger workers are guaranteed a slightly lower hourly rate of pay. Business owners found to be paying their workers below minimum wage can be prosecuted and fined. The Government also runs job centres to help jobseekers find work.

Citizens of Commonwealth countries, aged 17 to 30, can work in the UK without work permits under the *Highly Skilled Migrant Policy or Working Holidaymaker Scheme*. See Chapter 1 for more on coming to the UK to work.

The right to a home

In theory, local authorities have a duty to provide homeless Britons with a roof over their heads. But, in reality, local authorities prioritise their housing efforts on those considered *vulnerable*. Typically, to be considered vulnerable you would be one or more of the following: pregnant, already have children, have a severe mental health problem, abused where you currently live, disabled, or elderly.

Young, childless, single people in good health are at the back of the queue as far as obtaining public housing is concerned.

Under the 1996 Housing Act, local authorities have a duty to provide vulnerable people with accommodation for a minimum of two years.

As an asylum seeker, you're entitled to temporary accommodation while your application to remain in the UK is processed. However, asylum seekers cannot work, which means that you have to make do on very limited State handouts. See Chapter 2 for more.

Building up a State pension and claiming benefits

After you become a British citizen and start working you contribute *National Insurance (NI)* payments. NI payments are the route to gaining the State pension and other benefits. Contribute enough NI payments and, when you reach age 65, you are entitled to claim a State pension. Make sufficient NI payments and if you lose your job or become disabled you can claim Jobseekers Allowance and Incapacity Benefit.

For more on pensions and benefits, check out the Department for Work and Pensions' (DWP) Web site at www.dwp.gov.uk.

Getting Your Hands on a British Passport

As a British citizen you're entitled to a shiny new British passport. Owning a passport is a pretty big deal, because a British passport allows you to travel to other countries in the European Union without the need to apply for a visa, as well as to many other nations around the globe.

As well as allowing you to travel abroad, a passport acts as identification. It's increasingly important that you possess a ready means of proving your identity. For example, internal flight operators now ask for photo ID before allowing you to board a plane.

A British passport doesn't automatically grant you entry into *every* other country. Some nations demand that you obtain a visa and other documentation, such as medical or vaccination certificates, before allowing you in.

Applying for a passport

You can pick up an application form for a UK passport from your local Post Office. The form is straightforward. You're asked for the following information:

- Your personal details and those of your parents, such as your date of birth.

- Details of your certificate of naturalisation or registration as a British citizen, including the certificate number and place of issue.

- Two photographs of yourself, countersigned by a person of standing in the community such as a police officer, doctor, teacher, solicitor, or minister of religion.

  The person countersigning your photographs must be a British or Irish passport holder.

- A fee of £66 for a first-time British passport.

For more details on any aspect of getting hold of a passport, call the UK identity and passport agency helpline on 0870 521 0410.

If you're applying for your first British passport, you may want to use the Post Office's *check and send* passport service. For a fee of £7, the Post Office examines your form and photograph for any anomalies that can lead to your application being rejected.

Allow at least three weeks for an application for a passport sent through the post to be processed. If you need a passport sooner than that, you have to make an appointment at a passport service office. If you want a passport processed fast, you have to pay a larger fee than if you simply go through the postal, or check-and- send route.

Say cheese! Taking a passport photograph

The UK passport agency recently adopted a tough new approach to applicants' photographs because of enhanced security and immigration checking purposes. The upshot is that people failing to meet the agency's exacting standards have their applications rejected and have to reapply.

Here are a few golden rules of passport photographs:

- ✔ Your hair must be brushed away from your face and no shadow must fall on your face.

- ✔ No smiling – yes, that's right, I said no smiling!

- ✔ The picture must be 45 millimetres high and 35 millimetres wide.

- ✔ You must take the picture against an off-white, cream, or light grey plain background.

- ✔ The photograph must be a close-up shot of your head and shoulders. The distance from your chin to the crown of your head needs to be be between 29 and 34 millimetres in the photograph.

You've been told!

You can find photo booths in many Post Offices and shopping centres, and lots of photo processing shops can also take passport photos for you.

Chapter 7

Ten Helpful *For Dummies* Books

● ●

In This Chapter

▶ Delving into British, Irish, and European history

▶ Buying a property in the UK

▶ Starting your own business

▶ Knowing your legal rights

▶ Holding your own at a cricket match

● ●

A *For Dummies* book isn't complete without a fun and informative Part of Tens – a concise list of topical information at your fingertips.

This chapter gives you a taster of all the *For Dummies* titles available for you to get your hands on if you want to find out more about pretty much any aspect of living and working in the beautiful British Isles.

All the books in this chapter are published by Wiley and are available from libraries and bookshops nationwide. You can also order them online at www.wiley.co.uk.

British History For Dummies

Written by an Oxford-educated history teacher, *British History For Dummies* by Sean Lang is a fascinating and funny whistle-stop tour through the centuries of British history, from the Stone Age through to the present day.

If you want to know more about the class system in Britain, the significance of the royal family, or the importance of politics in British life, this book is for you.

If British history piques your interest and you want to find out more about the UK's influence in a wider context, see Sean Lang's *European History For Dummies*.

London For Dummies

When you arrive in the UK, your first port of call is likely to be one of the airports in London, and because the Embassies, Home Office, and immigration service are all based there, you're sure to spend some time in the Big Smoke (London).

London is a fast-moving city – a modern capital steeped in history. You may well need a helping hand to navigate not only the city itself, but also the currency you use and travel options you have (such as the famous black taxis and the underground rail system known as the Tube).

London For Dummies by Donald Olsen is a mine of information about the distinctive culture of London, along with must-see sights and experiences. You may also be interested in Donald Olsen's *England For Dummies*.

Buying a Home on a Budget For Dummies

Settling down in the UK almost certainly means eventually buying your own place. *Buying a Home on a Budget For Dummies*, by finance expert Melanie Bien, is a no-nonsense guide to getting on the property ladder for less.

You'll be amazed at how many options are open to first-time buyers; from pitching in with friends or family, to getting help from your local housing authority. Melanie Bien covers both the legal and practical aspects of becoming a homeowner in the UK, without the use of jargon or estate-agent speak!

When you come to selling a property in the UK, check out Melanie Bien's *Buying and Selling a Home For Dummies*.

Starting a Business For Dummies

After becoming a British citizen, you want to contribute to the country that has welcomed you to its green and pleasant land. If you're a bit of an entrepreneur, why not join the 400,000 others starting up their own business?

Colin Barrow, a seasoned entrepreneur himself, explains all you need to know to make a success of your start-up venture, from preparing a business plan to show to potential investors, to becoming a great manager when you reach the heady heights of employing people to work for you.

After you get your business off the ground, a good accompaniment to this book is Liz Barclay's *Small Business Employment Law For Dummies*.

Tough Interview Questions For Dummies

Starting your own business may not be one of the pressing goals in your life. But you still want to find a good job in the UK, right?

Rob Yeung's book is a lifesaver for anyone who wants to be thoroughly prepared when it comes to answering questions to a potential employer who you want to impress.

You may also want to check out *CVs For Dummies* by Steve Shipside and Joyce Lain Kennedy.

UK Law and Your Rights For Dummies

UK Law and Your Rights For Dummies offers invaluable information and advice for all UK citizens. What rights do you have if you want to return a faulty kettle? What can you do if your partner decides to leave you and take your CD collection? What can you do if your neighbour shouts offensive remarks to you every time you open the front door?

Liz Barclay explains everyday legal issues without resorting to mind-boggling jargon. The book shows you how to navigate legal bureaucracy and avoid ending up on the wrong side of the law.

Sorting Out Your Finances For Dummies

When you move to Britain, you move to a land renowned for its financial institutions. The Bank of England is the second oldest bank in the entire world – it was founded in 1694!

If you buy a property in the UK you're probably going to take out a mortgage, and you may have debts to pay off (after paying all those citizenship fees!), or decide you want to start putting some savings aside for the future.

Sorting Out Your Finances For Dummies by finance whizz Melanie Bien covers a huge range of money matters, from finding the best insurance to getting yourself set up with a pension.

Genealogy Online For Dummies

If you become a British citizen and go on to have children, you may want your kids to know their heritage and history. Although *Genealogy For Dummies* by Jenny Thomas, April Leigh Helm, Matthew L Helm, and Nick Barratt, is mainly geared for families with ancestors in Britain, you too may find it useful as a starting point for using your computer and the Internet to travel back in time through the centuries.

English Grammar For Dummies

If you want to improve your spoken and written English, *English Grammar For Dummies* by Lesley J Ward and

Geraldine Woods is the book for you. Written in plain English, and chock-full of useful examples, this guide explains everything from verbs, apostrophes, and commas, to pronouns, adverbs, and participles.

If you're writing letters, filling out application forms, or simply want to improve your spoken English, take a look at this book.

Cricket For Dummies

Written by yours truly, a lifelong fan and captain of two national championship teams, if you really want to immerse yourself in authentic British culture, this title is a must.

Say the word 'England' and many people instantly think of a pristine village green, with lean men in white clothes, bowling and batting with reserved determination. More English than tea with milk, *Cricket For Dummies* covers the rules of the game, tips on improving your play, and deciphers cricket-speak so you know your googly from your gully!

Part II
Revision Material

'To make sure he's going to a good
home, I'm going to have to give
you an English test.'

In this part...

The Home Office published a book called *Life in the United Kingdom: A Journey to Citizenship* on which the Life in the UK test is based. This part consists of the chapters you need to read and digest to pass the test. Covering politics, history, customs, everyday needs, education, work, and with a fair few statistics thrown in for good measure, read this part to immerse yourself in all things British.

Chapter 8

Revision Material for the Life in the UK Test

● ●

*T*he five chapters here are taken from the UK Government publication *Life in the United Kingdom: A Journey to Citizenship*. These chapters (2, 3, 4, 5, and 6) are the only part of the Government publication that you're examined on in the Life in the UK test, which you have to pass to gain British citizenship. If you do want to buy the whole book, you can purchase it from the Government's stationery office for £9.99. Check out www.tsoshop.co.uk for more details.

Read this appendix carefully and memorise as much of the content as you can. Appendix B consists of sample questions (and answers!) in the same vein as the questions you'll be asked in the test.

For more information about the test itself, visit www.lifeintheuktest.gov.uk.

Chapter 2: A Changing Society

Migration to Britain

Many people living in Britain today have their origins in other countries. They can trace their roots to regions throughout the world such as Europe, the Middle East, Africa, Asia, and the Caribbean. In the distant past, invaders came to Britain, seized land, and stayed. More recently, people come to Britain to find safety, jobs, and a better life.

Britain is proud of its tradition of offering safety to people who are escaping persecution and hardship. For example, in the 16th and 18th centuries, Huguenots (French Protestants) came to Britain to escape religious persecution in France. In the mid-1840s there was a terrible famine in Ireland and many Irish people migrated to Britain. Many Irish men became labourers, and helped to build canals and railways across Britain.

From 1880 to 1910, a large number of Jewish people came to Britain to escape racist attacks (called 'pogroms') in what was then called the Russian Empire, and from the countries now called Poland, Ukraine, and Belarus.

Migration since 1945

After the Second World War (1939–45), there was a huge task of rebuilding Britain. There were not enough people to do the work, so the British government encouraged workers from Ireland and other parts of Europe to come to the UK to help with the reconstruction. In 1948, people from the West Indies were also invited to come and work.

During the 1950s, there was still a shortage of labour in the UK. The UK encouraged immigration in the 1950s for economic reasons and many industries advertised for workers from overseas. For example, centres were set up in the West Indies to recruit people to drive buses. Textile and engineering firms from the north of England and the Midlands sent agents to India and Pakistan to find workers. For about 25 years, people from the West Indies, India, Pakistan, and later Bangladesh, travelled to work and settle in Britain.

The number of people migrating from these areas fell in the late 1960s because the government passed new laws to restrict immigration to Britain, although immigrants from 'old' Commonwealth countries such as Australia, New Zealand and Canada did not have to face such strict controls. During this time, however, Britain did admit 28,000 people of Indian origin who had been forced to leave Uganda, and 22,000 refugees from South-east Asia.

In the 1980s the largest immigrant groups came from the United States, Australia, South Africa, and New Zealand. In the early 1990s, groups of people from the former Soviet Union came to Britain looking for a new and safer way of life. Since 1994 there has been a global rise in mass migration for both political and economic reasons.

The Changing Role of Women

In 19th-century Britain, families were usually large and in many poorer homes men, women, and children all contributed towards the family income. Although they made an important economic contribution, women in Britain had fewer rights than men. Until 1857, a married woman had no right to divorce her husband. Until 1882, when a woman got married, her earnings, property, and money automatically belonged to her husband.

In the late 19th and early 20th centuries, an increasing number of women campaigned and demonstrated for greater rights and, in particular, the right to vote. They became known as 'Suffragettes'. These protests decreased during the First World War because women joined in the war effort and therefore did a much greater variety of work than they had before. When the First World War ended in 1918, women over the age of 30 were finally given the right to vote and to stand for election to Parliament. It was not until 1928 that women won the right to vote at 21, at the same age as men.

Despite these improvements, women still faced discrimination in the workplace. For example, it was quite common for employers to ask women to leave their jobs when they got married. Many jobs were closed to women and it was difficult for women to enter universities. During the 1960s and 1970s there was increasing pressure from women for equal rights. Parliament passed new laws giving women the right to equal pay, and prohibiting employers from discriminating against women because of their sex.

Women in Britain today

Women in Britain today make up 51 per cent of the population and 45 per cent of the workforce. These days, girls leave school, on average, with better qualifications than boys, and there are now more women than men at university.

Employment opportunities for women are now much greater than they were in the past. Although women continue to be employed in traditional female areas such as healthcare, teaching, secretarial, and retail work, there is strong evidence that attitudes are changing, and women are now active in a much wider range of work than before. Research shows that very few people today believe that women in Britain should stay at home and not go out to work. Today, almost three-quarters of women with school-age children are in paid work.

In most households, women continue to have the main responsibility for childcare and housework. There is evidence that there is now greater equality in homes and that more men are taking some responsibility for raising the family and doing housework. Despite this progress, many people believe that more needs to be done to achieve greater equality for women. There are still examples of discrimination against women, particularly in the workplace, despite the laws that exist to prevent it.

Women still do not always have the same access to promotion and better-paid jobs. The average hourly pay rate for women is 20 per cent less than for men, and after leaving university, most women still earn less than men.

Children, Family, and Young People

In the UK, there are almost 15 million children and young people up to the age of 19. This is almost onequarter of the UK population.

Over the last 20 years, family patterns in Britain have been transformed because of changing attitudes towards divorce and separation. Today, 65 per cent of children live with both birth parents, almost 25 per cent live in lone-parent families, and 10 per cent live within a step family. Most children in Britain receive weekly pocket money from their parents, and many get extra money for doing jobs around the house.

Children in the UK do not play outside the home as much as they did in the past. Part of the reason for this is increased home entertainment such as television, videos, and computers. There is also increased concern for children's safety and there are many stories in newspapers about child molestation by strangers, but there is no evidence that this kind of danger is increasing.

Young people have different identities, interests, and fashions to older people. Many young people move away from their family home when they become adults, but this varies from one community to another.

Education

The law states that children between the ages of 5 and 16 must attend school. The tests that pupils take are very important, and in England and Scotland children take national tests in English, mathematics, and science when they are 7, 11, and 14 years old. (In Wales, teachers assess children's progress when they are 7 and 11 and they take a national test at the age of 14). The tests give important information about children's progress and achievement, the subjects they are doing well in, and the areas where they need extra help.

Most young people take the General Certificate of Secondary Education (GCSE), or, in Scotland, Scottish Qualifications Authority (SQA) Standard Grade examinations when they are 16. At 17 and 18, many take vocational qualifications, General Certificates of Education at an Advanced level (AGCEs), AS level units or Higher/Advanced Higher Grades in Scotland. Schools and colleges expect good GCSE or SQA Standard Grade results before allowing a student to enrol on an AGCE or Scottish Higher/Advanced Higher course.

AS levels are Advanced Subsidiary qualifications gained by completing three AS units. Three AS units are considered as onehalf of an AGCE. In the second part of the course, three more AS units can be studied to complete the AGCE qualification.

Many people refer to AGCEs by the old name of A levels. AGCEs are the traditional route for entry to higher education courses, but many higher education students enter with different kinds of qualifications.

One in three young people now go on to higher education at college or university. Some young people defer their university entrance for a year and take a 'gap year'. This year out of education often includes voluntary work and travel overseas. Some young people work to earn and save money to pay for their university fees and living expenses.

People over 16 years of age may also choose to study at Colleges of Further Education or Adult Education Centres. There is a wide range of academic and vocational courses available as well as courses that develop leisure interests and skills. Contact your local college for details

Work

It is common for young people to have a part-time job while they are still at school. It is thought there are two million children at work at any one time. The most common jobs are newspaper delivery and work in super-markets and newsagents. Many parents believe that part-time work helps children to become more independent as well as providing them (and sometimes their families) with extra income.

There are laws about the age when children can take up paid work (usually not before 14), the type of work they can do, and the number of hours they can work (see www.worksmart.org.uk for more information).

It is very important to note that there are concerns for the safety of children who work illegally or who are not properly supervised, and the employment of children is strictly controlled by law.

Health hazards

Many parents worry that their children may misuse drugs and addictive substances.

✔ **Smoking:** Although cigarette smoking has fallen in the adult population, more young people are smoking, and more girls smoke than boys. By law, it is illegal to sell tobacco products to anyone under 16 years old. In some areas, smoking in public buildings and work environments is not allowed.

✔ **Alcohol:** Young people under the age of 18 are not allowed to buy alcohol in Britain, but there is concern about the age some young people start drinking alcohol and the amount of alcohol they drink at one time, known as 'binge drinking'. It is illegal to be drunk in public and there are now more penalties to help control this problem, including on-the-spot fines.

✔ **Illegal drugs:** As in most countries, it is illegal to possess drugs such as heroin, cocaine, ecstasy, amphetamines, and cannabis. Current statistics show that half of all young adults, and about a third of the population as a whole, have used illegal drugs at one time or another.

There is a strong link between the use of hard drugs (for example, crack cocaine and heroin) and crime, and also between hard drugs and mental illness. The misuse of drugs has a huge social and financial cost for the country. This is a serious issue and British society needs to find an effective way of dealing with the problem.

Young people's political and social attitudes

Young people in Britain can vote in elections from the age of 18. In the 2001 general election, however, only one in five first-time voters used their vote. There has been a great debate over the reasons for this. Some researchers think that one reason is that young people are not interested in the political process.

Although most young people show little interest in party politics, there is strong evidence that many are interested in specific political issues such as the environment and cruelty to animals.

In 2003 a survey of young people in England and Wales showed that they believe the five most important issues in Britain were crime, drugs, war/ terrorism, racism, and health. The same survey asked young people about their participation in political and community events. They found that 86 per cent of young people had taken part in some form of community event over the past year, and 50 per cent had taken part in fund-raising or collecting money for charity. Similar results have been found in surveys in Scotland and Northern Ireland. Many children first get involved in these activities while at school where they study Citizenship as part of the National Curriculum.

Chapter 3: UK Today: A Profile

Population

In 2005 the population of the United Kingdom was just under 60 million people.

UK population 2005:

- ✔ England (84% of the population) 50.1 million

- ✔ Scotland (8% of the population) 5.1 million

- ✔ Wales (5% of the population) 2.9 million

- ✔ N. Ireland (3% of the population) 1.7 million

- ✔ Total UK 59.8 million

Source: National Statistics

The population has grown by 7.7 per cent since 1971, and growth has been faster in more recent years. Although the general population in the UK has increased in the last 20 years, in some areas such as the North-east and North-west of England there has been a decline.

Both the birth rate and the death rate are falling and as a result the UK now has an ageing population. For instance, there are more people over 60 than children under 16. There is also a record number of people aged 85 and over.

The census

A census is a count of the whole population. It also collects statistics on topics such as age, place of birth, occupation, ethnicity, housing, health, and marital status.

A census has been taken every ten years since 1801, except during the Second World War. The next census will take place in 2011.

During a census, a form is delivered to every household in the country. This form asks for detailed information about each member of the household and must be completed by law. The information remains confidential and anonymous; it can only be released to the public after 100 years, when many people researching their family history find it very useful. General census information is used to identify population trends, and to help planning. More information about the census, the census form, and statistics from previous censuses, can be found at www. statistics.gov.uk/census.

Ethnic diversity

The UK population is ethnically diverse and is changing rapidly, especially in large cities such as London, so it is not always easy to get an exact picture of the ethnic origin of all the population from census statistics. Each of the four countries of the UK (England, Wales, Scotland, and Northern Ireland) has different customs, attitudes, and histories.

People of Indian, Pakistani, Chinese, Black Caribbean, Black African, Bangladeshi, and mixed ethnic descent make up 8.3 per cent of the UK population. Today about half the members of these communities were born in the United Kingdom.

There are also considerable numbers of people resident in the UK who are of Irish, Italian, Greek and Turkish Cypriot, Polish, Australian, Canadian, New Zealand, and American descent. Large numbers have also arrived since 2004 from the new East European member states of the European Union. These groups are not identified separately in the census statistics in the following list.

UK population 2001:

- White (including people of European, Australian, American descent): 54.2 million (92% UK population)

- Mixed: 0.7 million (1.2% UK population)

- Chinese: 0.2 million (0.4% UK population)

- Other: 0.2 million (0.4% UK population)

Asian or Asian British:

- Indian: 1.1 million (1.8% UK population)

- Pakistani: 0.7 million (1.3% UK population)

- Bangladeshi: 0.3 million (0.5% UK population)

- Other Asian: 0.2 million (0.4% UK population)

Black or Black British

- Black Caribbean: 0.6 million 1.0% UK population
- Black African: 0.5 million 0.8% UK population
- Black other: 0.1 million 0.2% UK population

Source: National Statistics from the 2001 census

Where do the largest ethnic minority groups live?

The figures from the 2001 census show that most members of the large ethnic minority groups in the UK live in England, where they make up 9 per cent of the total population. 45 per cent of all ethnic minority people live in the London area, where they form nearly one-third of the population (29 per cent). Other areas of England with large ethnic minority populations are the West Midlands, the South East, the North West, and Yorkshire and Humberside.

Proportion of ethnic minority groups in the countries of the UK:

- England: 9%
- Scotland: 2%
- Wales: 2%
- Northern Ireland: less than 1%

The nations and regions of the UK

The UK is a medium-sized country. The longest distance on the mainland, from John O'Groats on the north coast of Scotland to Land's End in the south-west corner of England, is about 870 miles (approximately 1,400 kilometres). Most of the population live in towns and cities.

There are many variations in culture and language in the different parts of the United Kingdom. This is seen in differences in architecture, in some local customs, in types of food, and especially in language. The English language has many accents and dialects, which give a clear indication of regional differences in the UK. Well-known dialects in England are Geordie (Tyneside), Scouse (Liverpool), and Cockney (London). Many other languages in addition to English are spoken in the UK, especially in multicultural cities.

In Wales, Scotland, and Northern Ireland, people speak different varieties and dialects of English. In Wales, too, an increasing number of people speak Welsh, which is taught in schools and universities. In Scotland, Gaelic is spoken in some parts of the Highlands and Islands, and in Northern Ireland a few people speak Irish Gaelic. Some of the dialects of English spoken in Scotland show the influence of the old Scottish language, Scots. One of the dialects spoken in Northern Ireland is called Ulster Scots.

Religion

Although the UK is historically a Christian society, everyone has the legal right to practise the religion of their choice. In the 2001 census, just over 75 per cent said they had a religion: seven out of ten of these were Christians. There were also a considerable number of people who followed other religions. Although many people in the UK said they held religious beliefs, currently only around 10 per cent of the population attend religious services. More people attend services in Scotland and Northern Ireland than in England and Wales. In London the number of people who attend religious services is increasing.

Religions in the UK:

✔ Christian (10% of whom are Roman Catholic): 71.6%

✔ Muslim: 2.7%

✔ Hindu: 1.0%

✔ Sikh: 0.6%

✔ Jewish: 0.5%

✔ Buddhist: 0.3%

✔ Other: 0.3%

✔ Total All: 77%

✔ No religion: 15.5%

✔ Not stated: 7.3%

Source: National Statistics from the 2001 census

The Christian Churches

In England there is a constitutional link between church and state. The official church of the state is the Church of England. The Church of England is called the Anglican Church in other countries and the Episcopal Church in Scotland, and in the USA. The Church of England is a Protestant church and has existed since the Reformation in the 1530s. The king or queen (the monarch) is the head, or Supreme Governor, of the Church of England. The monarch is not allowed to marry anyone who is not Protestant. The spiritual leader of the Church of England is the Archbishop of Canterbury. The monarch has the right to select the Archbishop and other senior church officials, but usually the choice is made by the Prime Minister and a committee appointed by the Church. Several Church of England bishops sit in the House of

Lords. In Scotland, the established church is the Presbyterian Church; its head is the Chief Moderator. There is no established church in Wales, or in Northern Ireland.

Other Protestant Christian groups in the UK are Baptists, Presbyterians, Methodists, and Quakers. 10 per cent of Christians are Roman Catholic (40 per cent in Northern Ireland).

Patron saints

England, Scotland, Wales, and Northern Ireland each have a national saint called a patron saint. Each saint has a feast day. In the past these were celebrated as holy days when many people had a day off work. Today these are not public holidays except for 17 March in Northern Ireland.

Patron saints' days:

- ✔ St David's day, Wales 1 March
- ✔ St Patrick's day, Northern Ireland 17 March
- ✔ St George's day, England 23 April
- ✔ St Andrew's day, Scotland 30 November

There are also four public holidays a year called Bank Holidays. They are of no religious or national significance.

Customs and Traditions

Festivals

Throughout the year there are festivals of art, music, and culture, such as the Notting Hill Carnival in west London and the Edinburgh Festival. Customs and traditions from various religions, such as Eid ul-Fitr (Muslim), Diwali

(Hindu), and Hanukkah (Jewish) are widely recognised in the UK. Children learn about these at school. The main Christian festivals are Christmas and Easter. There are also celebrations of non-religious traditions such as New Year.

- ✔ **Christmas Day:** 25 December, celebrates the birth of Jesus Christ. It is a public holiday. Many Christians go to church on Christmas Eve (24 December) or on Christmas Day itself. Christmas is also usually celebrated by people who aren't Christian. People usually spend the day at home and eat a special meal, which often includes turkey. They give each other gifts, send each other cards, and decorate their houses. Many people decorate a tree. Christmas is a special time for children. Very young children believe that an old man, Father Christmas (or Santa Claus), brings them presents during the night. He is always shown in pictures with a long white beard, dressed in red. Boxing Day, 26 December, is the day after Christmas. It is a public holiday.

- ✔ **New Year:** 1 January, is a public holiday. People usually celebrate on the night of 31 December. In Scotland, 31 December is called Hogmanay, and 2 January is also a public holiday. In Scotland Hogmanay is a bigger holiday for some people than Christmas.

- ✔ **Valentine's Day:** 14 February, is when lovers exchange cards and gifts. Sometimes people send anonymous cards to someone they secretly admire.

- ✔ **April Fool's Day:** 1 April, is a day when people play jokes on each other until midday. Often TV and newspapers carry stories intended to deceive credulous viewers and readers.

- **Mother's Day:** The Sunday three weeks before Easter is a day when children send cards or buy gifts for their mothers. Easter is also an important Christian festival.

- **Hallowe'en:** 31 October, is a very ancient festival. Young people often dress up in frightening costumes to play 'trick or treat'. Giving them sweets or chocolates might stop them playing a trick on you. Sometimes people carry lanterns made out of pumpkins with a candle inside.

- **Guy Fawkes Night:** 5 November, is an occasion when people in Great Britain set off fireworks at home or in special displays. The origin of this celebration was an event in 1605, when a group of Catholics, led by Guy Fawkes, failed in its plan to kill the Protestant king with a bomb in the Houses of Parliament.

- **Remembrance Day:** 11 November, commemorates those who died fighting in World War 1, World War 2 and other wars. Many people wear poppies (a red flower) in memory of those who died. At 11 a.m. there is a two-minute silence.

Sport

Sport of all kinds plays a important part in many people's lives. Football, tennis, rugby, and cricket are very popular sports in the UK. There are no United Kingdom teams for football and rugby. England, Scotland, Wales, and Northern Ireland have their own teams. Important sporting events include, the Grand National horse race, the Football Association (FA) cup final (and equivalents in Northern Ireland, Scotland, and Wales), the Open golf championship, and the Wimbledon tennis tournament.

Chapter 4: How the United Kingdom is Governed

The British Constitution

As a constitutional democracy, the United Kingdom is governed by a wide range of institutions, many of which provide checks on each other's powers. Most of these institutions are of long standing: they include the monarchy, Parliament, (consisting of the House of Commons and the House of Lords), the office of Prime Minister, the Cabinet, the judiciary, the police, the civil service, and the institutions of local government. More recently, devolved administrations have been set up for Scotland, Wales, and Northern Ireland. Together, these formal institutions, laws, and conventions form the British Constitution. Some people would argue that the roles of other less formal institutions, such as the media and pressure groups, should also be seen as part of the Constitution.

The British Constitution is not written down in any single document, as are the constitutions of many other countries. This is mainly because the United Kingdom has never had a lasting revolution, like America or France, so our most important institutions have been in existence for hundreds of years. Some people believe that there should be a single document, but others believe that an unwritten constitution allows more scope for institutions to adapt to meet changing circumstances and public expectations.

The monarchy

Queen Elizabeth II is the Head of State of the United Kingdom. She is also the monarch or Head of State for many countries in the Commonwealth. The UK, like

Denmark, the Netherlands, Norway, Spain, and Sweden, has a constitutional monarchy. This means that the king or queen does not rule the country, but appoints the government that the people have chosen in democratic elections. Although the queen or king can advise, warn, and encourage the Prime Minister, the decisions on government policies are made by the Prime Minister and Cabinet.

The Queen has reigned since her father's death in 1952. Prince Charles, the Prince of Wales, her eldest son, is the heir to the throne.

The Queen has important ceremonial roles such as the opening of the new parliamentary session each year. On this occasion the Queen makes a speech that summarises the government's policies for the year ahead.

Government

The system of government in the United Kingdom is a parliamentary democracy. The UK is divided into 646 parliamentary constituencies and at least every five years, voters in each constituency elect their Member of Parliament (MP) in a general election. All of the elected MPs form the House of Commons. Most MPs belong to a political party and the party with the largest number of MPs forms the government.

The law that requires new elections to Parliament to be held at least every five years is so fundamental that no government has sought to change it. A Bill to change it is the only one to which the House of Lords must give its consent.

Some people argue that the power of Parliament is lessened because of the obligation on the United Kingdom to accept the rules of the European Union and the judgments of the European Court, but it was Parliament itself that created these obligations.

The House of Commons

The House of Commons is the more important of the two chambers in Parliament, and its members are democratically elected. Nowadays the Prime Minister and almost all the members of the Cabinet are members of the House of Commons. The members of the House of Commons are called 'Members of Parliament' or MPs for short. Each MP represents a parliamentary constituency, or area of the country: there are 646 of these. MPs have a number of different responsibilities. They represent everyone in their constituency, they help to create new laws, they scrutinise and comment on what the government is doing, and they debate important national issues.

Elections

There must be a general election to elect MPs at least every five years, though they may be held sooner if the Prime Minister so decides. If an MP dies or resigns, another election, called a by-election, is called in his or her constituency. MPs are elected through a system called 'first past the post'. In each constituency, the candidate who gets the most votes is elected. The government is then formed by the party that wins the majority of constituencies.

The Whips

The Whips are a small group of MPs appointed by their party leaders. They are responsible for discipline in their party, and for making sure MPs attend the House of Commons to vote. The Chief Whip often attends Cabinet or Shadow Cabinet meetings and arranges the schedule of proceedings in the House of Commons with the Speaker.

European parliamentary elections

Elections for the European Parliament are also held every five years. There are 78 seats for representatives from the UK in the European Parliament and elected members are called Members of the European Parliament (MEPs). Elections to the European Parliament use a system of proportional representation, whereby seats are allocated to each party in proportion to the total votes it won.

The House of Lords

Members of the House of Lords, known as peers, are not elected and do not represent a constituency. The role and membership of the House of Lords have recently undergone big changes. Until 1958 all peers were either 'hereditary', meaning that their titles were inherited, senior judges, or bishops of the Church of England. Since 1958 the Prime Minister has had the power to appoint peers just for their own lifetime. These peers, known as Life Peers, have usually had a distinguished career in politics, business, law, or some other profession. This means that debates in the House of Lords often draw on more specialist knowledge than is available to members of the House of Commons. Life Peers are appointed by the Queen on the advice of the Prime Minister, but they include people nominated by the leaders of the other main parties and by an independent Appointments Commission for non-party peers.

In the last few years the hereditary peers have lost the automatic right to attend the House of Lords, although they are allowed to elect a few of their number to represent them.

While the House of Lords is usually the less important of the two chambers of Parliament, it is more independent of the government. It can suggest amendments or propose new laws, which are then discussed by the House of

Commons. The House of Lords can become very important if the majority of its members will not agree to pass a law for which the House of Commons has voted. The House of Commons has powers to overrule the House of Lords, but these are very rarely used.

The Prime Minister

The Prime Minister (PM) is the leader of the political party in power. He or she appoints the members of the Cabinet and has control over many important public appointments. The official home of the Prime Minister is 10 Downing Street, in central London, near the Houses of Parliament; he or she also has a country house not far from London called Chequers. The Prime Minister can be changed if the MPs in the governing party decide to do so, or if he or she wishes to resign. More usually, the Prime Minister resigns when his or her party is defeated in a general election.

The Cabinet

The Prime Minister appoints about 20 senior MPs to become ministers in charge of departments. These include the Chancellor of the Exchequer, responsible for the economy, the Home Secretary, responsible for law, order and immigration, the Foreign Secretary, and ministers (called 'Secretaries of State') for education, health, and defence. The Lord Chancellor, who is the minister responsible for legal affairs, is also a member of the Cabinet, but sat in the House of Lords rather than the House of Commons. Following legislation passed in 2005, it is now possible for the Lord Chancellor to sit in the Commons. These ministers form the Cabinet, a small committee that usually meets weekly and makes important decisions about government policy, which often then needs to be debated or approved by Parliament.

The Opposition

The second largest party in the House of Commons is called the Opposition. The Leader of the Opposition is the person who hopes to become Prime Minister if his or her party wins the next general election. The Leader of the Opposition leads his or her party in pointing out the government's failures and weaknesses; one important opportunity to do this is at Prime Minister's Questions, which takes place every week while Parliament is sitting. The Leader of the Opposition also appoints senior Opposition MPs to lead the criticism of government ministers, and together they form the Shadow Cabinet.

The Speaker

Debates in the House of Commons are chaired by the Speaker, who is the chief officer of the House of Commons. The Speaker is politically neutral. He or she is an MP, elected by fellow MPs to keep order during political debates and to make sure the rules are followed. This includes making sure the Opposition has a guaranteed amount of time to debate issues it chooses. The Speaker also represents Parliament at ceremonial occasions.

The party system

Under the British system of parliamentary democracy, anyone can stand for election as an MP but they are unlikely to win an election unless they have been nominated to represent one of the major political parties. These are the Labour Party, the Conservative Party, the Liberal Democrats, or one of the parties representing Scottish, Welsh, or Northern Irish interests. There are just a few MPs who do not represent any of the main political parties and are called 'independents'. The main political parties actively seek members among ordinary voters to join their debates, contribute to their costs, and help at elections for Parliament or for local government; they have branches in most constituencies, and they hold policy-making conferences every year.

Pressure and lobby groups

Pressure and lobby groups are organisations that try to influence government policy. They play a very important role in politics. There are many pressure groups in the UK. They may represent economic interests (such as the Confederation of British Industry, the Consumers' Association, or the trade unions) or views on particular subjects (for example, Greenpeace or Liberty). The general public is more likely to support pressure groups than join a political party.

The civil service

Civil servants are managers and administrators who carry out government policy. They have to be politically neutral and professional, regardless of which political party is in power. Although civil servants have to follow the policies of the elected government, they can warn ministers if they think a policy is impractical or not in the public interest. Before a general election takes place, top civil servants study the Opposition party's policies closely in case they need to be ready to serve a new government with different aims and policies.

Devolved administration

In order to give people in Wales and Scotland more control of matters that directly affect them, in 1997 the government began a programme of devolving power from central government. Since 1999 there has been a Welsh Assembly, a Scottish Parliament and, periodically, a Northern Ireland Assembly. Although policy and laws governing defence, foreign affairs, taxation, and social security all remain under central UK government control, many other public services now come under the control of the devolved administrations in Wales and Scotland.

Both the Scottish Parliament and Welsh Assembly have been set up using forms of proportional representation, which ensures that each party gets a number of seats in proportion to the number of votes they receive. Similarly, proportional representation is used in Northern Ireland in order to ensure 'power sharing' between the Unionist majority (mainly Protestant) and the substantial (mainly Catholic) minority aligned to Irish nationalist parties. A different form of proportional representation is used for elections to the European Parliament.

The Welsh Assembly Government

The National Assembly for Wales, or Welsh Assembly Government (WAG), is situated in Cardiff, the capital city of Wales. It has 60 Assembly Members (AMs) and elections are held every four years. Members can speak in either Welsh or English, and all its publications are in both languages. The Assembly has the power to make decisions on important matters such as education policy, the environment, health services, transport, and local government, and to pass laws for Wales on these matters within a statutory framework set out by the UK Parliament at Westminster.

The Parliament of Scotland

A long campaign in Scotland for more independence and democratic control led to the formation in 1999 of the Parliament of Scotland, which sits in Edinburgh, the capital city of Scotland.

There are 129 Members of the Scottish Parliament (MSPs), elected by a form of proportional representation. This has led to the sharing of power in Scotland between the Labour and Liberal Democrat parties. The Scottish Parliament can pass legislation for Scotland on all matters that are not specifically reserved to the UK Parliament.

The matters on which the Scottish Parliament can legislate include civil and criminal law, health, education, planning, and the raising of additional taxes.

The Northern Ireland Assembly

A Northern Ireland Parliament was established in 1922 when Ireland was divided, but it was abolished in 1972 shortly after the Troubles broke out in 1969.

Soon after the end of the Troubles, the Northern Ireland Assembly was established with a power-sharing agreement, which distributes ministerial offices among the main parties. The Assembly has 108 elected members known as MLAs (Members of the Legislative Assembly). Decision-making powers devolved to Northern Ireland include education, agriculture, the environment, health, and social services in Northern Ireland.

The UK government kept the power to suspend the Northern Ireland Assembly if the political leaders no longer agreed to work together, or if the Assembly was not working in the interests of the people of Northern Ireland. This has happened several times and the Assembly is currently suspended (2006). This means that the elected assembly members do not have power to pass bills or make decisions.

Local government

Towns, cities, and rural areas in the UK are governed by democratically elected councils, often called local authorities. Some areas have both district and county councils, which have different functions, although most larger towns and cities have a single local authority. Many councils representing towns and cities appoint a mayor who is the ceremonial leader of the council, but in some towns a mayor is appointed to be the effective leader of the administration. London has 33 local authorities, with the

Greater London Authority and the Mayor of London coordinating policies across the capital. Local authorities are required to provide 'mandatory services' in their area. These services include education, housing, social services, passenger transport, the fire service, rubbish collection, planning, environmental health, and libraries.

Most of the money for the local authority services comes from the government through taxes. Only about 20 per cent is funded locally through 'council tax', a local tax set by councils to help pay for local services. It applies to all domestic properties, including houses, bungalows, flats, maisonettes, mobile homes, or houseboats, whether owned, or rented.

Local elections for councillors are held in May every year. Many candidates stand for council election as members of a political party.

The judiciary

In the UK the laws made by Parliament are the highest authority. But often important questions arise about how the laws are to be interpreted in particular cases. It is the task of the judges (who are together called 'the judiciary') to interpret the law, and the government may not interfere with their role. Often the actions of the government are claimed to be illegal and, if the judges agree, then the government must either change its policies or ask Parliament to change the law. This has become all the more important in recent years, as the judges now have the task of applying the Human Rights Act. If they find that a public body is not respecting a person's human rights, they may order that body to change its practices and to pay compensation, if appropriate. If the judges believe that an Act of Parliament is incompatible with the Human Rights Act, they cannot change it themselves, but they can ask Parliament to consider doing so.

Judges cannot, however, decide whether people are guilty or innocent of serious crimes. When someone is accused of a serious crime, a jury decides whether he or she is innocent or guilty and, if guilty, the judge then decides on the penalty. For less important crimes, a magistrate decides on guilt, and on any penalty.

The police

The police service is organised locally, with one police service for each county or group of counties. The largest force is the Metropolitan Police, which serves London and is based at New Scotland Yard. Northern Ireland as a whole is served by the Police Service for Northern Ireland (PSNI). The police have 'operational independence', which means that the government cannot instruct them on what to do in any particular case. But the powers of the police are limited by the law and their finances are controlled by the government and by police authorities made up of councillors and magistrates. The Independent Police Complaints Commission (or, in Northern Ireland, the Police Ombudsman) investigates serious complaints against the police.

Non-departmental public bodies (quangos)

Non-departmental public bodies, also known as quangos, are independent organisations that carry out functions on behalf of the public that would be inappropriate to place under the political control of a Cabinet minister. There are many hundreds of these bodies, carrying out a wide variety of public duties. Appointments to these bodies are usually made by ministers, but they must do so in an open and fair way.

The role of the media

Proceedings in Parliament are broadcast on digital television and published in official reports such as Hansard, which is available in large libraries and on the Internet:

www.parliament.uk. Most people, however, get information about political issues and events from newspapers (often called the press), television, and radio.

The UK has a free press, meaning that what is written in newspapers is free from government control. Newspaper owners and editors hold strong political opinions and run campaigns to try and influence government policy and public opinion. As a result it is sometimes difficult to distinguish fact from opinion in newspaper coverage.

By law, radio and television coverage of the political parties at election periods must be balanced and so equal time has to be given to rival viewpoints. But broadcasters are free to interview politicians in a tough and lively way.

Who can vote?

The United Kingdom has had a fully democratic system since 1928, when women were allowed to vote at 21, the same age as men. The present voting age of 18 was set in 1969, and (with a few exceptions, such as convicted prisoners) all UK-born and naturalised citizens have full civic rights, including the right to vote and do jury service.

Citizens of the UK, the Commonwealth and the Irish Republic (if resident in the UK) can vote in all public elections. Citizens of EU states who are resident in the UK can vote in all elections except national parliamentary (general) elections.

In order to vote in a parliamentary, local, or European election, you must have your name on the register of electors, known as the electoral register. If you are eligible to vote, you can register by contacting your local council election registration office. If you don't know what your local authority is, you can find out by telephoning the Local Government Association (LGA) information line on 020

7664 3131 between 9 a.m. and 5 p.m., Monday to Friday. You must tell them your postcode or your full address, and they can then give you the name of your local authority. You can also get voter registration forms in English, Welsh, and some other languages, on the Internet: www. electoralcommission.org.uk.

The electoral register is updated every year in September or October. An electoral registration form is sent to every household and it has to be completed and returned, with the names of everyone who is resident in the household and eligible to vote on 15 October.

In Northern Ireland a different system operates. This is called individual registration and all those entitled to vote must complete their own registration form. Once registered, you can stay on the register provided your personal details do not change. For more information telephone the Electoral Office for Northern Ireland on 028 9044 6688.

By law, each local authority has to make its electoral register available for anyone to look at, although this now has to be supervised. The register is kept at each local electoral registration office (or council office in England and Wales). It is also possible to see the register at some public buildings such as libraries.

Standing for office

Most citizens of the United Kingdom, the Irish Republic, or the Commonwealth, who are aged 18 or over, can stand for public office. There are some exceptions and these include members of the armed forces, civil servants, and people found guilty of certain criminal offences. Members of the House of Lords may not stand for election to the House of Commons but are eligible for all other public offices.

To become a local councillor, a candidate must have a local connection with the area through work, being on the electoral register, or through renting or owning land or property.

Contacting elected members

All elected members have a duty to serve and represent their constituents. You can get contact details for all your representatives and their parties from your local library. Assembly members, MSPs, MPs, and MEPs are also listed in the phone book and Yellow Pages. You can contact MPs by letter, or phone, at their constituency office or their office in the House of Commons: The House of Commons, Westminster, London SW1A 0AA, or telephone: 020 7729 3000. Many Assembly Members, MSPs, MPs, and MEPs hold regular local 'surgeries'. These are often advertised in the local paper and constituents can go and talk about issues in person. You can find out the name of your local MP and get in touch with them by fax through the Web site: www.writetothem.com. This service is free.

How to visit Parliament and the Devolved Administrations

The public can listen to debates in the Palace of Westminster from public galleries in both the House of Commons and the House of Lords. You can either write to your local MP in advance to ask for tickets or you can queue on the day at the public entrance. Entrance is free. Sometimes there are long queues for the House of Commons and you may have to wait for at least one or two hours. It is usually easier to get into the House of Lords. You can find further information on the UK Parliament Web site: www.parliament.uk.

In Northern Ireland, elected members, known as MLAs, meet in the Northern Ireland Assembly at Stormont, in Belfast. The Northern Ireland Assembly is presently suspended. There are two ways to arrange a visit to Stormont. You can either contact the Education Service (details on the Northern Ireland Assembly Web site: www. niassembly.gov.uk) or contact an MLA.

In Scotland, the elected members, called MSPs, meet in the Scottish Parliament at Holyrood in Edinburgh (for more information see: www.scottish.parliament.uk). You can get information, book tickets, or arrange tours through the visitor services. You can write to them at The Scottish Parliament, Edinburgh, EH99 1SP, or telephone: 0131 348 5200, or email sp.bookings@scottish. parliament.uk.

In Wales, the elected members, known as AMs, meet in the Welsh Assembly in the Senedd in Cardiff Bay (for more information see: www.wales.gov.uk). You can book guided tours or seats in the public galleries for the Welsh Assembly. To make a booking, telephone the Assembly booking line on 029 2089 8477 or email: assembly. booking@wales.gsi.gov.uk.

The UK in Europe and the World

The Commonwealth

The Commonwealth is an association of countries, most of which were once part of the British Empire, though a few countries that weren't in the Empire have also joined it.

Commonwealth Members

Antigua and Barbuda	Lesotho
Australia	Malawi
The Bahamas	Malaysia
Bangladesh	Maldives
Barbados	Malta
Belize	Mauritius
Botswana	Mozambique
Brunei Darussalam	Namibia
Cameroon	Nauru[*]
Canada	New Zealand
Cyprus	Nigeria
Dominica	Pakistan
Fiji Islands	Papua New Guinea
The Gambia	St Kitts and Nevis
Ghana	St Lucia
Grenada	St Vincent and the Grenadines
Guyana	Samoa
India	Seychelles
Jamaica	Sierra Leone
Kenya	Singapore
Kiribati	Solomon Islands

(continued)

Commonwealth Members	
South Africa	Uganda
Sri Lanka	United Kingdom
Swaziland	United Republic of Tanzania
Tonga	Vanuatu
Trinidad and Tobago	Zambia
Tuvalu	

*Nauru is a Special Member.

The Queen is the head of the Commonwealth, which currently has 53 member states. Membership is voluntary and the Commonwealth has no power over its members although it can suspend membership. The Commonwealth aims to promote democracy, good government, and to eradicate poverty.

The European Union (EU)

The European Union (EU), originally called the European Economic Community (EEC), was set up by six Western European countries who signed the Treaty of Rome on 25 March 1957. One of the main reasons for doing this was the belief that cooperation between states would reduce the likelihood of another war in Europe. Originally the UK decided not to join this group, and only became part of the European Union in 1973. In 2004, ten new member countries joined the EU, with a further two in 2006 making a total of 27 member countries.

One of the main aims of the EU today is for member states to function as a single market. Most of the countries of the EU have a shared currency, the euro, but the

UK has decided to retain its own currency unless the British people choose to accept the euro in a referendum. Citizens of an EU member state have the right to travel to, and work in, any EU country if they have a valid passport or identity card. This right can be restricted on the grounds of public health, public order, and public security. The right to work is also sometimes restricted for citizens of countries that have joined the EU recently.

The Council of the European Union (usually called the Council of Ministers) is effectively the governing body of the EU. It is made up of government ministers from each country in the EU and, together with the European Parliament, is the legislative body of the EU. The Council of Ministers passes EU law on the recommendations of the European Commission and the European Parliament and takes the most important decisions about how the EU is run. The European Commission is based in Brussels, the capital city of Belgium. It is the civil service of the EU and drafts proposals for new EU policies and laws, and administers its funding programmes.

The European Parliament meets in Strasbourg, in northeastern France, and in Brussels. Each country elects members, called Members of the European Parliament (MEPs), every five years. The European Parliament examines decisions made by the European Council and the European Commission, and it has the power to refuse agreement to European laws proposed by the Commission and to check on the spending of EU funds.

European Union law is legally binding in the UK and all the other member states. European laws, called directives, regulations, or framework decisions, have made a lot of difference to people's rights in the UK, particularly at work. For example, there are EU directives about the procedures for making workers redundant, and regulations that limit the number of hours people can be made to work.

The Council of Europe

The Council of Europe was created in 1949 and the UK was one of the founder members. Most of the countries of Europe are members. It has no power to make laws but draws up conventions and charters, which focus on human rights, democracy, education, the environment, health, and culture. The most important of these is the European Convention on Human Rights; all member states are bound by this Convention, and a member state which persistently refuses to obey the Convention may be expelled from the Council of Europe.

The United Nations (UN)

The UK is a member of the United Nations (UN), an international organisation to which over 190 countries now belong. The UN was set up after the Second World War and aims to prevent war and promote international peace and security. There are 15 members on the UN Security Council, which recommends action by the UN when there are international crises and threats to peace. The UK is one of the five permanent members.

Three very important agreements produced by the UN are the Universal Declaration of Human Rights, the Convention on the Elimination of All Forms of Discrimination against Women, and the UN Convention on the Rights of the Child. Although none of these has the force of law, they are widely used in political debate and legal cases, both to reinforce the law and to assess the behaviour of countries.

Chapter 5: Everyday Needs

Housing

Buying a home

Two-thirds of people in the UK own their own home. Most other people rent houses, flats, or rooms.

Mortgages

People who buy their own home usually pay for it with a mortgage, or a special loan from a bank or building society. This loan is paid back, with interest, over a long period of time, usually 25 years. You can get information about mortgages from a bank or building society. Some banks can also give information about Islamic (Sharia) mortgages.

If you are having problems paying your mortgage repayments, you can get help and advice. It is important to speak to your bank or building society as soon as you can.

Estate agents

If you wish to buy a home, usually the first place to start is an estate agent. In Scotland the process is different and you should go first to a solicitor. Estate agents represent the person selling their house or flat. They arrange for buyers to visit homes that are for sale. There are estate agents in all towns and cities and they usually have Web sites where they advertise the homes for sale. You can also find details about homes for sale on the Internet and in national, and local, newspapers.

Making an offer

In the UK, except in Scotland, when you find a home you wish to buy you have to make an offer to the seller. You usually do this through an estate agent or solicitor. Many people offer a lower price than the seller is asking. Your first offer must be 'subject to contract' so that you can withdraw if there are reasons why you cannot complete the purchase. In Scotland, the seller sets a price and buyers make offers over that amount. The agreement becomes legally binding earlier than it does elsewhere in the UK.

Solicitor and surveyor

It is important that a solicitor helps you through the process of buying a house or flat. When you make an offer on a property, the solicitor carries out a number of legal checks on the property, the seller, and the local area. The solicitor provides the legal agreements necessary for you to buy the property. The bank or building society that is providing you with your mortgage also carries out checks on the house or flat you wish to buy. These particular checks are done by a surveyor. The buyer does not usually see the result of this survey, so the buyer often asks a second surveyor to check the house as well. In Scotland the survey is carried out before an offer is made, to help people decide how much they want to bid for the property.

Rented accommodation

It is possible to rent accommodation from the local authority (the council), from a housing association, or from private property owners called landlords.

The local authority

Most local authorities (or councils) provide housing. This is often called 'council housing'. In Northern Ireland social housing is provided by the Northern Ireland Housing Executive (www.nihe.co.uk). In Scotland you can find information on social housing at: www.sfha.co.uk. Everyone is entitled to apply for council accommodation.

To apply you must put your name on the council register or list. This is available from the housing department at the local authority. You are then assessed according to your needs. This is done through a system of points. You get more points if you have priority needs, for example, if you are homeless and have children, or chronic ill health.

It is important to note that in many areas of the UK there is a shortage of council accommodation, and that some people have to wait a very long time for a house or flat.

Housing associations

Housing associations are independent not-for-profit organisations that provide housing for rent. In some areas they have taken over the administration of local authority housing. They also run schemes called shared ownership, which help people buy part of a house or flat if they cannot afford to buy all of it at once. There are usually waiting lists for homes owned by housing associations.

Privately rented accommodation

Many people rent houses or flats privately, from land-lords. Information about private accommodation can be found in local newspapers, notice boards, estate agents, and letting agents.

Tenancy agreement

When you rent a house or flat privately you sign a ten-ancy agreement, or lease. This explains the conditions or 'rules' you must follow while renting the property. This agreement must be checked very carefully to avoid problems later. The agreement also contains a list of any furniture or fittings in the property. This is called an inventory. Before you sign the agreement, check the details and keep it safe during your tenancy.

Deposit and rent

You are usually asked to give the landlord a deposit at the beginning of your tenancy. This is to cover the cost of any damage. It is usually equal to one month's rent. The landlord must return this money to you at the end of your tenancy, unless you have caused damage to the property.

Your rent is fixed with your landlord at the beginning of the tenancy. The landlord cannot raise the rent without your agreement.

If you have a low income, or are unemployed, you may be able to claim Housing Benefit to help you pay your rent.

Renewing and ending a tenancy

Tenancy agreements are for a fixed period of time, often six months. After this time the tenancy can be ended or, if both tenant and landlord agree, renewed. If you end the tenancy before the fixed time, you usually have to pay the rent for the agreed full period of the tenancy.

A landlord cannot force a tenant to leave. If a landlord wishes a tenant to leave they must follow the correct procedures. These vary according to the type of tenancy. It is a criminal offence for a landlord to use threats or violence against a tenant, or to force them to leave without an order from court.

Discrimination

It is unlawful for a landlord to discriminate against someone looking for accommodation because of their sex, race, nationality, or ethnic group, or because they are disabled, unless the landlord, or a close relative of the landlord, is sharing the accommodation.

Homelessness

If you are homeless you should go for help to the local authority (or, in Northern Ireland, the Housing Executive). They have a legal duty to offer help and advice, but cannot offer you a place to live unless you have priority need (see above) and have a connection with the area, such as work or family. You must also show that you have not made yourself intentionally homeless.

Help

If you are homeless or have problems with your landlord, help can be found from the following:

- ✔ The housing department of the local authority gives advice on homelessness and on Housing Benefit as well as deal with problems you may have in council-owned property.

- ✔ The Citizen's Advice Bureau gives advice on all types of housing problems. There may also be a housing advice centre in your neighbourhood.

- ✔ Shelter is a housing charity which runs a 24-hour helpline on 0808 800 4444, or visit www.shelternet. org.uk.

- ✔ Help with the cost of moving and setting up home may be available from the Social Fund. This is run by the Department for Work and Pensions (DWP). It provides grants and loans such as the Community Care Grant for people setting up home after being homeless, or after they have been in prison or other institutions. Other loans are available for people who have had an emergency such as flooding. Information about these is available at the Citizen's Advice Bureau or Jobcentre Plus.

Services In and For the Home

Water

Water is supplied to all homes in the UK. The charge for this is called the water rates. When you move in to a new home (bought or rented), you should receive a letter telling you the name of the company responsible for supplying your water. The water rates may be paid in one payment (a lump sum) or in instalments, usually monthly. If you receive Housing Benefit, you should check to see if this covers the water rates. The cost of the water usually depends on the size of your property, but some homes have a water meter, which tells you exactly how much water you have used. In Northern Ireland water is currently included in the domestic rates, although this may change in future.

Electricity and gas

All properties in the UK have electricity supplied at 240 volts. Most homes also have gas. When you move into a new home, or leave an old one, you should make a note of the electricity and gas meter readings. If you have an urgent problem with your gas, electricity, or water supply, you can ring a 24-hour helpline. This can be found on your bill, in the Yellow Pages, or in the phone book.

Gas and electricity suppliers

It is possible to choose between different gas and electricity suppliers. These have different prices and different terms and conditions. Get advice before you sign a contract with a new supplier. To find out which company supplies your gas, telephone Transco on 0870 608 1524

To find out which company supplies your electricity, telephone Energywatch on 0845 906 0708, or visit: www. energywatch.org.uk. Energywatch can also give you advice on changing your supplier of electricity or gas.

Telephone

Most homes already have a telephone line (called a land line). If you need a new line, telephone BT on 150 442, or contact a cable company. Many companies offer landline, mobile telephone, and broadband Internet services. You can get advice about prices or about changing your company from Ofcom at: www.ofcom.org.uk. You can call from public payphones using cash, pre-paid phonecards, or credit or debit cards. Calls made from hotels and hostels are usually more expensive. Dial 999 or 112 for emergency calls for police, fire, or ambulance service. These calls are free. Do not use these numbers if it is not a real emergency; you can always find the local numbers for these services in the phone book.

Bills

On the back of each bill, you can find information on how to pay for your water, gas, electricity, and the telephone. If you have a bank account you can pay your bills by standing order or direct debit. Most companies operate a budget scheme, which allows you to pay a fixed sum every month. If you do not pay a bill, the service can be cut off. To get a service reconnected, you have to pay another charge.

Refuse collection

Refuse is also called waste, or rubbish. The local authority collects the waste regularly, usually on the same day of each week. Waste must be put outside in a particular place to get collected. In some parts of the country the waste is put into plastic bags, in others it is put into bins with wheels. In many areas you have to recycle your rubbish, separating paper, glass, metal, or plastic, from the other rubbish. Large objects that you want to throw away, such as a bed, a wardrobe, or a fridge, need to be collected separately. Contact the local authority to arrange this. If you have a business, such as a factory or a shop, you must make special arrangements with the local authority for your waste to be collected. It is a criminal offence to dump rubbish anywhere.

Council Tax

Local government services, such as education, police, roads, refuse collection, and libraries, are paid for partly by grants from the government and partly by Council Tax. Northern Ireland operates a system of domestic rates, instead of the Council Tax. The amount of Council Tax you pay depends on the size and value of your house or flat (dwelling). You must register to pay Council Tax when you move into a new property, either as the owner or the tenant. You can pay the tax in one payment, in two instalments, or in ten instalments (from April to January).

If only one person lives in the flat or house, you get a 25 per cent reduction on your Council Tax. (This does not apply in Northern Ireland). You may also get a reduction if someone in the property has a disability. People on a low income, or who receive benefits such as Income Support or Jobseeker's Allowance, can claim Council Tax Benefit. You can get advice on this from the local authority, or the Citizen's Advice Bureau.

Buildings and household insurance

If you buy a home with a mortgage, you must insure the building against fire, theft, and accidental damage. The landlord should arrange insurance for rented buildings. It is also wise to insure your possessions against theft or damage. There are many companies that provide insurance.

Neighbours

If you live in rented accommodation, you have a tenancy agreement. This explains all the conditions of your tenancy. It probably also includes information on what to do if you have problems with your housing. Occasionally, there may be problems with your neighbours. If you do have problems with your neighbours, these can usually be solved by speaking to them first. If you cannot solve the problem, speak to your landlord, local authority, or housing association. Keep a record of the problems in case you have to show exactly what the problems are, and when they started. Neighbours who cause a very serious nuisance may be taken to court and can be evicted from their home.

There are several mediation organisations that help neighbours to solve their disputes without having to go to court. Mediators talk to both sides and try to find a solution acceptable to both. You can get details of mediation organisations from the local authority, Citizen's Advice Bureau, and Mediation UK on 0117 904 6661 or visit: www.mediationuk.co.uk.

Money and Credit

Bank notes in the UK come in denominations (values) of £5, £10, £20, and £50. Northern Ireland and Scotland have their own bank notes, which are valid everywhere in the UK, though sometimes people may not realise this, and may not agree to accept them.

The euro

In January 2002, twelve European Union (EU) states adopted the euro as their common currency. The UK government decided not to adopt the euro at that time, and has said it will only do so if the British people vote for the euro in a referendum. The euro does circulate to some extent in Northern Ireland, particularly in the towns near the border with Ireland.

Foreign currency

You can buy, or change, foreign currency at banks, building societies, large post offices, and exchange shops or bureaux de change. You might have to order some currencies in advance. The exchange rates vary and you should check for the best deal.

Banks and building societies

Most adults in the UK have a bank or building society account. Many large national banks or building societies have branches in towns and cities throughout the UK. It is worth checking the different types of account each one offers. Many employers pay salaries directly into a bank or building society account. There are many banks and building societies to choose from. To open an account, you need to show documents to prove your identity, such as a passport, immigration document, or driving licence. You also need to show something with your address on it like a tenancy agreement or household bill. It's also possible to open bank accounts in some supermarkets, or on the Internet.

Cash and debit cards

Cash cards allow you to use cash machines to withdraw money from your account. For this you need a Personal Identification Number (PIN), which you must keep secret. A debit card allows you to pay for things without using cash. You must have enough money in your account to cover what you buy. If you lose your cash card or debit card, you must inform the bank immediately.

Credit and store cards

Credit cards can be used to buy things in shops, on the telephone, and over the Internet. A store card is like a credit card but used only in a specific shop. Credit and store cards do not draw money from your bank account, but you are sent a bill every month. If you do not pay the total amount on the bill, you are charged interest. Although credit and store cards are useful, the interest is usually very high, and many people fall into debt this way. If you lose your credit or store cards you must inform the company immediately.

Credit and loans

People in the UK often borrow money from banks and other organisations to pay for things like household goods, cars, and holidays. This is more common in the UK than in many other countries. You must be very sure of the terms and conditions when you decide to take out a loan. You can get advice on loans from the Citizen's Advice Bureau if you're uncertain.

Being refused credit

Banks and other organisations use different information about you to make a decision about a loan, such as your occupation, address, salary, and previous credit record. If you apply for a loan you might be refused. If this happens, you have the right to ask the reason why.

Credit unions

Credit unions are financial co-operatives owned and controlled by their members. The members pool their savings and then make loans from this pool. Interest rates in credit unions are usually lower than banks and building societies. There are credit unions in many cities and towns. To find the nearest credit union contact the Association of British Credit Unions (ABCUL) on: www. abcul.coop.

Insurance

As well as insuring their property and possessions, many people insure their credit cards and mobile phones. They also buy insurance when they travel abroad in case they lose their luggage or need medical treatment. Insurance is compulsory if you have a car or motorcycle. You can usually arrange insurance directly with an insurance company, or you can use a broker to help you get the best deal.

Social security

The UK has a system of social security, which pays welfare benefits to people who do not have enough money to live on. Benefits are usually available for the sick and disabled, older people, the unemployed, and those on low incomes. People who do not have legal rights of residence (or 'settlement') in the UK cannot usually receive benefits. Arrangements for paying and receiving benefits are complex because they have to cover people in many different situations. Guides to benefits are available from Jobcentre Plus offices, local libraries, post offices, and the Citizen'sAdvice Bureau.

Health

Healthcare in the UK is organised under the National Health Service (NHS). The NHS began in 1948, and is one of the largest organisations in Europe. It provides all residents with free healthcare and treatment.

Finding a doctor

Family doctors are called General Practitioners (GPs) and they work in surgeries. GPs often work together in a group practice. This is sometimes called a Primary Health Care Centre.

Your GP is responsible for organising the health treatment you receive. Treatment can be for physical and mental illnesses. If you need to see a specialist, you must go to your GP first. Your GP then refers you to a specialist in a hospital. Your GP can also refer you for specialist treatment if you have special needs.

You can get a list of local GPs from libraries, post offices, the tourist information office, the Citizen's Advice Bureau, the local Health Authority, and from the following Web sites:

- ✔ www.nhs.uk/ for health practitioners in England
- ✔ www.wales.nhs.uk/directory.cfm for health practitioners in Wales
- ✔ www.n-i.nhs.uk for health practitioners in Northern Ireland
- ✔ www.show.scot.nhs.uk/findnearest/ healthservices in Scotland.

You can also ask neighbours and friends for the name of their local doctor.

You can attend a hospital without a GP's letter only in the case of an emergency. If you have an emergency you should go to the Accident and Emergency (A&E) department of the nearest hospital.

Registering with a GP

Look for a GP as soon as you move to a new area. Don't wait until you are ill. The health centre, or surgery, tells you what you need to do to register. Usually you must have a medical card. If you do not have one, the GP's receptionist should give you a form to send to the local health authority, which then sends you a medical card.

Before you register, check that the surgery can offer what you need. For example, you might need a woman GP, or maternity services. Sometimes GPs have many patients and are unable to accept new ones. If you cannot find a GP, you can ask your local health authority to help you find one.

Using your doctor

All patients registering with a GP are entitled to a free health check. Appointments to see the GP can be made by phone or in person. Sometimes you may have to wait several days before you can see a doctor. If you need immediate medical attention, ask for an urgent appointment. Arrive at the GP's surgery a few minutes before your appointment. If you cannot attend, or do not need the appointment any more, you must let the surgery know. The GP needs patients to answer all questions as fully as possible in order to find out what is wrong. Everything you tell the GP is completely confidential and cannot be passed on to anyone else without your permission. If you do not understand something, ask for clarification. If you have difficulties with English, bring someone who can help you, or ask the receptionist for an interpreter. This must be done when you make the appointment. If you have asked for an interpreter, it is especially important that you keep your appointment, because this service is expensive.

In exceptional circumstances, GPs can visit patients at home, but they always give priority to people who are unable to travel. If you call the GP outside normal working hours, you need to answer several questions about your situation. This is to assess how serious your case is. You're then told if a doctor can come to your home. You may be advised to go to the nearest A&E department.

Charges

Treatment from the GP is free but you have to pay a charge for your medicines, and for certain services, such as vaccinations for travel abroad. If the GP decides you need to take medicine, you're given a prescription. You must take this to a pharmacy (chemist).

Prescriptions

Prescriptions are free for anyone who is

- ✔ Under 16 years of age (under 25 in Wales)

- ✔ Under 19 and in full-time education

- ✔ Aged 60 or over

- ✔ Pregnant or with a baby under 12 months old

- ✔ Suffering from a specified medical condition

- ✔ Receiving Income Support, Jobseekers' Allowance, Working Families, or Disabilities Tax Credit

Feeling unwell

If you or your child feels unwell, you have the following options:

For information or advice:

- ✔ Ask your local pharmacist (chemist). The pharmacy can give advice on medicines, and about some illnesses and conditions that are not serious.

- ✔ Speak to a nurse by phoning NHS Direct on 0845 46 47.

- ✔ Use the NHS Direct Web site, NHS Direct Online: www.nhsdirect.nhs.uk.

To see a doctor or nurse:

- ✔ Make an appointment to see your GP or a nurse working in the surgery.
- ✔ Visit an NHS walk-in centre.

For urgent medical treatment:

- ✔ Contact your GP.
- ✔ Go to your nearest hospital with an Accident and Emergency department.
- ✔ Call 999 for an ambulance. Calls are free. *Only* use this service for a real emergency.

NHS Direct is a 24-hour telephone service that provides information on particular health conditions, telephone: 0845 46 47. You may ask for an interpreter for advice in your own language. In Scotland, NHS24 at: www.nhs24. com, telephone: 08454 24 24 24.

NHS Direct Online is a Web site providing information about health services and several medical conditions, and treatments: www.nhsdirect.nhs.uk.

NHS walk-in centres provide treatment for minor injuries and illnesses seven days a week. You do not need an appointment. For details of your nearest centre call NHS Direct or visit the NHS Web site at: www.nhs.uk (for Northern Ireland www.n-i.nhs.uk) and click on 'local NHS services'.

Going into hospital

If you need minor tests at a hospital, you may need to attend the Outpatients department. If your treatment takes several hours, you go into hospital as a day patient.

If you need to stay overnight, you go into hospital as an in-patient.

You should take personal belongings with you, such as a towel, night clothes, things for washing, and a dressing gown. You receive all your meals while you are an in-patient. If you need advice about going into hospital, contact Customer Services or the Patient Advice and Liaison Service (PALS) at the hospital where you're to receive treatment.

Dentists

You can find the name of a dentist by asking at the local library, at the Citizen's Advice Bureau and through NHS Direct. Most people have to pay for dental treatment. Some dentists work for the NHS and some are private. NHS dentists charge less than private dentists, but some dentists have two sets of charges, both NHS and private. A dentist should explain your treatment and the charges before the treatment begins.

Free dental treatment is available to:

- ✔ People under 18 (in Wales, people under 25 and over 60).
- ✔ Pregnant women and women with babies under 12 months old.
- ✔ People on income support, Jobseekers' Allowance or Pension Credit Guarantee.

Opticians

Most people have to pay for sight tests and glasses, except children, people over 60, people with particular eye conditions, and people receiving certain benefits. In Scotland, eye tests are free.

Pregnancy and care of young children

If you are pregnant you receive regular ante-natal care. This is available from your local hospital, local health centre, or from special antenatal clinics. You receive support from a GP and from a midwife. Midwives work in hospitals or health centres. Some GPs do not provide maternity services so you may wish to look for another GP during your pregnancy. In the UK, women usually have their babies in hospital, especially if it is their first baby. It is common for the father to attend the birth, but only if the mother wants him to be there.

A short time after you have your child, you begin regular contact with a health visitor. She or he is a qualified nurse and can advise you about caring for your baby. The first visits are in your home, but after that you might meet the health visitor at a clinic. You can ask advice from your health visitor until your child is five years old. In most towns and cities there are mother and toddler groups, or playgroups for small children. These often take place at local churches and community centres. You might be able to send your child to a nursery school.

Information on pregnancy

You can get information on maternity and ante-natal services in your area from your local health authority, a health visitor, or your GP. The number of your health authority is in the phone book.

The Family Planning Association (FPA) gives advice on contraception and sexual health. The FPA's helpline is 0845 310 1334, or: www.fpa.org.uk.

The National Childbirth Trust gives information and support in pregnancy, childbirth, and early parenthood: www.nctpregnancyandbabycare.com.

Registering a birth

Your must register your baby with the Registrar of Births, Marriages, and Deaths (Register Office) within six weeks of the birth. The address of your local Register Office is in the phone book. If the parents are married, either the mother or father can register the birth. If they are not married, only the mother can register the birth. If the parents are not married but want both names on the child's birth certificate, both mother and father must be present when they register their baby.

Education

Going to school

Education in the UK is free, and compulsory for all children between the ages of 5 and 16 (4 to 16 in Northern Ireland). The education system varies in England, Scotland, Wales, and Northern Ireland.

The child's parent or guardian is responsible for making sure their child goes to school, arrives on time, and attends for the whole school year. If they do not do this, the parent or guardian may be prosecuted.

Some areas of the country offer free nursery education for children over the age of 3. In most parts of the UK, compulsory education is divided into two stages, primary and secondary. In some places there is a middle-school system. In England and Wales the primary stage lasts from 5 to 11, in Scotland from 5 to 12 and in Northern Ireland from 4 to 11. The secondary stage lasts until the age of 16. At that age, young people can choose to leave school or to continue with their education until they are 17 or 18.

Details of local schools are available from your local education authority office or Web site. The addresses and phone numbers of local education authorities are in the phone book.

Primary schools

These are usually schools where both boys and girls learn together and are usually close to a child's home. Children tend to be with the same group and teacher all day. Schools encourage parents to help their children with learning, particularly with reading and writing.

Secondary schools

At age 11 (12 in Scotland) children go to secondary school. This might normally be the school nearest their home, but parents in England and Wales are allowed to express a preference for a different school. In some areas, getting a secondary school place in a preferred school can be difficult, and parents often apply to several schools in order to make sure their child gets offered a place. In Northern Ireland many schools select children through a test taken at the age of 11.

If the preferred school has enough places, the child is offered a place. If there are not enough places, children are offered places according to the school's admission arrangements. Admission arrangements vary from area to area.

Secondary schools are larger than primary schools. Most are mixed sex, although there are single sex schools in some areas. Your local education authority can give you information on schools in your area. It can also tell you which schools have spaces and give you information about why some children are given places when only a few are available, and why other children might not. It also tells you how to apply for a secondary school place.

Costs

Education at state schools in the UK is free, but parents have to pay for school uniforms and sports wear. There are sometimes extra charges for music lessons and for school outings. Parents on low incomes can get help with costs, and with the cost of school meals. You can get advice on this from the local education authority or the Citizen's Advice Bureau.

Church and other faith schools

Some primary and secondary schools in the UK are linked to the Church of England or the Roman Catholic Church. These are called 'faith schools'. In some areas there are Muslim, Jewish, and Sikh schools. In Northern Ireland, some schools are called Integrated Schools. These schools aim to bring children of different religions together. Information on faith schools is available from your local education authority.

Independent schools

Independent schools are private schools. They're not run or paid for by the state. Independent secondary schools are also sometimes called public schools. There are about 2,500 independent schools in the UK. About 8 per cent of children go to these schools. At independent schools, parents must pay the full cost of their child's education. Some independent schools offer scholarships, which pay some or all of the costs of the child's education.

The school curriculum

All state, primary, and secondary schools in England, Wales, and Northern Ireland follow the National Curriculum. This covers English, maths, science, design and technology, information and communication technology (ICT), history, geography, modern foreign languages, art and design, music, physical education (PE), and citizenship. In Wales, children learn Welsh.

In some primary schools in Wales, all the lessons are taught in Welsh. In Scotland, pupils follow a broad curriculum informed by national guidance. Schools must, by law, provide religious education (RE) to all pupils. Parents are allowed to withdraw their children from these lessons. RE lessons have a Christian basis, but children also learn about the other major religions.

Assessment

In England, the curriculum is divided into four stages, called Key Stages. After each stage children are tested. They take Key Stage tests (also called SATs) at ages 7, 11, and 14. At 16 they usually take the General Certificates of Secondary Education (GCSEs) in several subjects, although some schools also offer other qualifications. At 18, young people who have stayed at school do AGCEs (Advanced GCE levels), often just called A levels.

In Wales, schools follow the Welsh National Curriculum but have abolished national tests for children at age 7 and 11. There are also plans in Wales to stop testing children at 14. Teachers in Wales still have to assess and report on their pupils' progress and achievements at 7 and 11.

In Scotland, the curriculum is divided into two phases. The first phase is from 5 to 14. There are six levels in this phase, levels A to F. There are no tests for whole groups during this time. Teachers test individual children when they are ready. From 14 to 16, young people do Standard Grade. After 16 they can study at Intermediate, Higher, or Advanced level. In Scotland there is soon to be a single curriculum for all pupils from age 3 to age 18. This is called A Curriculum for Excellence. More information can be found at: www.acurriculumforexcellencescotland. gov.uk.

Help with English

If your child's main language is not English, the school may arrange for extra language support from an EAL (English Additional Language) specialist teacher.

Careers education

All children get careers advice from the age of 14. Advice is also available from Connexions, a national service for young people: telephone 080 800 13219 or: www. connexions-direct.com in England. In Wales, Careers Wales offers advice to children from the age of 11. For further information visit: www.careerswales.com or telephone 0800 100 900.

In Scotland, Careers Scotland provides information, services, and support to all ages and stages. For further information visit: www.careers-scotland.org.uk or telephone 0845 8 502 502.

Parents and schools

Many parents are involved with their child's school. A number of places on a school's governing body are reserved for parents. The governing body decides how the school is run and administered, and produces reports on the progress of the school from year to year. In Scotland, parents can be members of school boards or parent councils.

Schools must be open 190 days a year. Term dates are decided by the governing body or by the local education authority. Children must attend the whole school year. Schools expect parents and guardians to inform them if their child is going to be absent from school. All schools ask parents to sign a home-school agreement. This is a list of things that both the school and the parent or guardian agree to do to ensure a good education for the child. All parents receive a report every year on their child's progress. They also have the chance to go to the school to talk to their child's teachers.

Further education and adult education

At 16, young people can leave school or stay on to do A levels (Higher grades in Scotland) in preparation for university. Some young people go to their local further education (FE) college to improve their exam grades, or to get new qualifications for a career. Most courses are free up to the age of 19. Young people from families with low incomes can get financial help with their studies when they leave school at 16. This is called the Education Maintenance Allowance (EMA). Information about this is available at your local college or at: www.dfes.gov.uk.

Further education colleges also offer courses to adults over the age of 18. These include courses for people wishing to improve their skills in English. These courses are called ESOL (English for Speakers of Other Languages). There are also courses for English speakers who need to improve their literacy and numeracy, and for people who need to learn new skills for employment. ESOL courses are also available in community centres and training centres. There is sometimes a waiting list for ESOL courses because demand is high. In England and Wales, ESOL, literacy, and numeracy courses are also called Skills for Life courses. You can get information at your local college or local library or from learndirect on 0800 100 900.

Many people join other adult education classes to learn a new skill or hobby, and to meet new people. Classes are very varied and range from sports to learning a musical instrument, or a new language. Details are usually available from your local library, college, or adult education centre.

University

More young people go to university now than in the past. Many go after A levels (or Higher grades in Scotland) at age 18 but it is also possible to go to university later in life. At present, most students in England, Wales, and Northern Ireland have to pay towards the cost of their tuition fees and to pay for their living expenses. In Scotland there are no tuition fees but after students finish university they pay back some of the cost of their education in a payment called an endowment. At present, universities can charge up to £3,000 per year for their tuition fees, but students do not have to pay anything towards their fees before or during their studies. The government pays their tuition fees and then charges for them when a student starts working after university. Some families on low incomes receive help with their children's tuition fees. This is called a grant. The universities also give help, in the form of bursaries. Most students get a low-interest student loan from a bank. This pays for their living costs while they're at university. When a student finishes university and starts working, he or she must pay back the loan.

Leisure

Information

Information about theatre, cinema, music, and exhibitions is found in local newspapers, local libraries, and tourist information offices. Many museums and art galleries are free.

Film, video, and DVD

Films in the UK have a system to show if they are suitable for children. This is called the classification system. If a child is below the age of the classification, they may not watch the film at a cinema, or on DVD. All films receive a classification, as follows:

- ✓ **U** (Universal): suitable for anyone aged 4 years and over

- ✓ **PG** (parental guidance): suitable for everyone, but some parts of the film might be unsuitable for children. Their parents should decide.

- ✓ **12** or **12a**: children under 12 are not allowed to see or rent the film unless they are with an adult.

- ✓ **15**: children under 15 are not allowed to see or rent the film.

- ✓ **18**: no one under 18 is allowed to see or rent the film.

- ✓ **R18**: no one under 18 is allowed to see the film, which is only available in specially licensed cinemas.

Television and radio

Anyone in the UK with a television (TV), DVD or video recorder, computer, or any device that is used for watching or recording TV programmes, must be covered by a valid television licence. One licence covers all of the equipment at one address, but people who rent different rooms in a shared house must each buy a separate licence.

A colour TV licence currently costs £131.50 (2006) and lasts for 12 months. People aged 75, or over can apply for a free TV licence. Blind people can claim a 50 per cent discount on their TV licence. You risk prosecution and a fine if you watch TV but are not covered by a TV licence. There are many ways to buy a TV licence including from local Pay Point outlets or on-line at: www.tvlicensing.co.uk. It is also possible to pay for the licence in instalments. For more information telephone 0870 576 3763 or write to TV Licensing, Bristol, BS98 1TL.

Sports, clubs, and societies

Information about local clubs and societies can usually be found at local libraries, or through your local authority. For information about sports you should ask in the local leisure centre. Libraries and leisure centres often organise activities for children during the school holidays.

Places of interest

The UK has a large network of public footpaths in the countryside. Many parts of the countryside and places of interest are kept open by the National Trust. This is a charity that works to preserve important buildings and countryside in the UK. Information about National Trust buildings and areas open to the public is available on: www.nationaltrust.org.uk.

Pubs and night clubs

Public houses, or pubs, are an important part of social life in the UK. To drink alcohol in a pub you must be 18 or over. People under 18 are not allowed to buy alcohol in a supermarket, or in an off-licence. The landlord of the pub may allow people of 14 to come into the pub but they are not allowed to drink alcohol. At 16, people can drink wine or beer with a meal in a hotel or restaurant.

Pubs are usually open during the day and until 11 p.m. If a pub wants to stay open later, it must apply for a special licence. Nightclubs open and close later than pubs.

Betting and gambling

People under 18 are not allowed into betting shops or gambling clubs. There is a National Lottery for which draws, with large prizes, are made every week. You can enter by buying a ticket or a scratch card. People under 16 are not allowed to buy a lottery ticket or scratch card.

Pets

Many people in the UK have pets such as cats and dogs. It is against the law to treat a pet cruelly or to neglect it. All dogs in public places must wear a collar showing the name and address of the owner. The owner is responsible for keeping the dog under control, and for cleaning up after the animal in a public place. Vaccinations and medical treatment for animals are available from veterinary surgeons (vets). If you cannot afford to pay a vet, you can go to a charity called the PDSA (People's Dispensary for Sick Animals). To find your nearest branch, visit: www. pdsa.org.uk.

Travel and Transport

Trains, buses, and coaches

For information about trains, telephone the National Rail Enquiry Service: 08457 48 49 50, or visit: www. nationalrail.co.uk. For trains in Northern Ireland, phone Translink on 028 90 66 66 30 or visit: www. translink.co.uk. For information about local bus times phone 0870 608 250. For information on coaches, telephone National Express on 08705 80 80 80, or visit: www. nationalexpress.com. For coaches in Scotland, telephone Scottish Citylink on 08705 50 50 50 or visit: www. citylink.co.uk. For Northern Ireland, visit: www. translink.co.uk.

Usually, tickets for trains and underground systems such as the London Underground must be bought before you get on the train. The fare varies according to the day and time you wish to travel. Travelling in the rush hour is always more expensive. Discount tickets are available for families, people aged 60 and over, disabled people, students, and people under 26. Ask at your local train station for details. Failure to buy a ticket may result in a penalty.

Taxis

To operate legally, all taxis and minicabs must be licensed and display a licence plate. Taxis and cabs with no licence are not insured for fare-paying passengers and are not always safe. Women should not use unlicensed minicabs.

Driving

You must be at least 17 to drive a car or motorcycle, 18 to drive a medium-sized lorry, and 21 to drive a large lorry or bus. To drive a lorry, minibus, or bus with more than eight passenger seats, you must have a special licence.

The driving licence

You must have a driving licence to drive on public roads. To get a driving licence you must pass a test. There are many driving schools where you can learn with the help of a qualified instructor.

You get a full driving licence in three stages:

1. **Apply for a provisional licence.** You need this licence while you are learning to drive. With this you are allowed to drive a motorcycle up to 125cc or a car. You must put L plates on the vehicle, or D plates in Wales. Learner drivers cannot drive on a motorway. If you drive a car, you must be with someone who is over 21 and who has held a full licence for over three years. You can get an application form for a provisional licence from a post office.

2. **Pass a written theory test.**

3. **Pass a practical driving test.**

Drivers may use their licence until they are 70. After that the licence is valid for three years at a time.

In Northern Ireland, a newly qualified driver must display an R-Plate (for registered driver) for one year after passing the test.

Overseas licences

If your driving licence is from a country in the European Union (EU), Iceland, Liechtenstein, or Norway, you can drive in the UK for as long as your licence is valid.

If you have a licence from a country outside the EU, you may use it in the UK for up to 12 months. During this time you must get a UK provisional driving licence and pass both the UK theory and practical driving tests, or you are not permitted to drive after the 12-month period.

Insurance

It is a criminal offence to have a car without proper motor insurance. Drivers without insurance can receive very high fines. It is also illegal to allow someone to use your car if they are not insured to drive it.

Road tax and MOT

You must also pay a tax to drive your car on the roads. This is called road tax. Your vehicle must have a road tax disc which shows you've paid. You can buy this at the post office. If you do not pay the road tax, your vehicle may be clamped or towed away.

If your vehicle is over three years old, you must take it every year for a Ministry of Transport (MOT) test. You can do this at an approved garage. The garage gives you an MOT certificate when your car passes the test. It is an offence not to have an MOT certificate. If you do not have an MOT certificate, your insurance is not be valid.

Safety

Everyone in a vehicle should wear a seat belt. Children under 12 years of age may need a special booster seat. Motorcyclists and their passengers must wear a crash helmet (this law does not apply to Sikh men if they are wearing a turban). It is illegal to drive while holding a mobile phone.

Speed limits

For cars and motorcycles the speed limits are:

- 30 miles per hour (mph) in built-up areas, unless a sign shows a different limit; 60 mph on single carriageways
- 70 mph on motorways and dual carriageways

Speed limits are lower for buses, lorries, and cars pulling caravans.

It is illegal to drive when you are over the alcohol limit, or drunk. The police can stop you and test you to see how much alcohol you have in your body. This is called a breathalyser test. If a driver has more than the permitted amount of alcohol (called being 'over the limit') or refuses to take the test, he or she is arrested. People who drink and drive can expect to be disqualified from driving for a long period.

Accidents

If you are involved in a road accident:

1. **Don't drive away without stopping – this is a criminal offence.**

2. **Call the police and ambulance on 999 or 112 if someone is injured.**

3. **Get the names, addresses, vehicle registration numbers, and insurance details of the other drivers.**

4. **Give your details to the other drivers or passengers, and to the police.**

5. **Make a note of everything that happened and contact your insurance company as soon as possible.**

Note that if you admit the accident was your fault, the insurance company may refuse to pay. It's better to wait until the insurance company decides for itself whose fault the accident was.

Identity documents

At present, UK citizens do not have to carry identity (ID) cards. The government is, however, making plans to introduce them in the next few years.

Proving your identity

You may have to prove your identity at different times, such as when you open a bank account, rent accommodation, enrol for a college course, hire a car, apply for benefits such as housing benefit, or apply for a marriage certificate. Different organisations may ask for different documents as proof of identity. These can include

- ✔ Official documents from the Home Office showing your immigration status

- ✔ A certificate of identity

- ✔ A passport or travel document

- ✔ A National Insurance (NI) number card

- ✔ A provisional or full driving licence

> ✔ A recent gas, electricity or phone bill showing your name and address
>
> ✔ A rent or benefits book

Chapter 6: Employment

Looking for Work

If you are looking for work, or you are thinking of changing your job, there are a number of ways you can find out about work opportunities. The Home Office provides guidance on who is allowed to work in the UK. Not everyone in the UK is allowed to work, and some people need work permits, so it is important to check your status before taking up work. Also, employers have to check that anyone they employ is legally entitled to work in the UK. For more information and guidance, see the Home Office Web site 'Working in the UK' at www.workingintheuk.gov.uk.

Jobs are usually advertised in local and national newspapers, at the local Jobcentre and in employment agencies. You can find the address and telephone number of your local Jobcentre under Jobcentre Plus in the phone book or see: www.jobcentreplus.gov.uk. Some jobs are advertised on supermarket notice boards and in shop windows. These jobs are usually part-time and the wages are often quite low. If there are particular companies you would like to work for, you can look for vacancies on their Web sites.

Jobcentre Plus is run by a government department – the Department for Work and Pensions. Trained staff give advice and help in finding and applying for jobs, as well as claiming benefits. They can also arrange for interpreters. Their Web site www.jobcentreplus.gov.uk lists vacancies and training opportunities and gives general information on benefits. There is also a low cost telephone service – Jobseeker Direct, telephone: 0845 60 60 234. This is open 9 a.m. to 6 p.m. on weekdays and 9 a.m. to 1 p.m. on Saturdays.

Qualifications

Applicants for some jobs need special training or qualifications. If you have qualifications from another country, you can find out how they compare with qualifications in the UK at the National Academic Recognition Information Centre (NARIC), www.naric.org.uk.

For further information contact UK NARIC, ECCTIS Ltd, Oriel House, Oriel Road, Cheltenham Glos, GL50 1XP, telephone: 0870 990 4088, email: info@naric.org.uk.

Applications

Interviews for lower paid and local jobs can often be arranged by telephone or in person. For many jobs you need to fill in an application form or send a copy of your curriculum vitae (CV) with a covering letter, or letter of application.

A covering letter is usually a short letter attached to a completed application form, while a letter of application gives more detailed information on why you are applying for the job and why you think you are suitable. Your CV gives specific details on your education, qualifications, previous employment, skills, and interests. It is important to type any letters, and your CV, on a computer or word processor as this improves your chance of being called for an interview.

Employers often ask for the names and addresses of one or two referees. These are people such as your current or previous employer or college tutor. Referees need to know you well and to agree to write a short report or reference on your suitability for the job. Personal friends or members of your family are not normally acceptable as referees.

Interviews

In job descriptions and interviews, employers should give full details of what the job involves, including the pay, holidays, and working conditions. If you need more information about any of these, you can ask questions in the interview. In fact, asking some questions in the interview shows you are interested and can improve your chance of getting the job. When you are applying for a job, and during the interview, it is important to be honest about your qualifications and experience. If an employer later finds out that you gave incorrect information, you might lose your job.

Criminal record

For some jobs, particularly if the work involves working with children or vulnerable people, the employer asks for your permission to do a criminal record check. You can get more information on this from the Home Office Criminal Records Bureau (CRB) information line, telephone: 0870 90 90 811. In Scotland, contact Disclosure Scotland: www.disclosurescotland.co.uk. Helpline: 0870 609 6006.

Training

Taking up training helps people improve their qualifications for work. Some training may be offered at work or you can do courses from home, or at your local college. This includes English language training. You can get more information from your local library and college, or from Web sites such as www.worktrain.gov.uk and www.learndirect.co.uk. Learndirect offers a range of online training courses at centres across the country. There are charges for courses, but you can do free starter or taster sessions. You can get more information from their free information and advice line, telephone: 0800 100 900.

Volunteering and work experience

Some people do voluntary work and this can be a good way to support your local community and organisations, which depend on volunteers. It also provides useful experience that can help with future job applications. Your local library has information about volunteering opportunities.

You can also get information and advice from Web sites such as: www.do-it.org.uk, www.volunteering.org.uk, and www.justdosomething.net.

Equal Rights and Discrimination

It is against the law for employers to discriminate against someone at work. This means that a person should not be refused work, training, or promotion, or be treated less favourably because of their:

- Sex
- Nationality, race, colour, or ethnic group
- Disability
- Religion
- Sexual orientation
- Age

In Northern Ireland, the law also bans discrimination on grounds of religious belief or political opinion.

The law also says that men and women who do the same job, or work of equal value, should receive equal pay. Almost all the laws protecting people at work apply equally to people doing part-time or full-time jobs.

There are, however, a small number of jobs where discrimination laws do not apply. For example, discrimination is not against the law when the job involves working for someone in his or her own home.

You can get more information about the law and racial discrimination from the Commission for Racial Equality. The Equal Opportunities Commission can help with sex discrimination issues and the Disability Rights Commission deals with disability issues. Each of these organisations offers advice and information and can, in some cases, support individuals. From October 2007 their functions are to be brought together in a new Commission for Equality and Human Rights. You can get more information about the laws protecting people at work from the Citizen's Advice Bureau Web site: www.adviceguide.org.uk.

In Northern Ireland, the Equality Commission provides information and advice in respect of all forms of unlawful discrimination.

The Commission for Racial Equality, St Dunstan's House, 201–211 Borough High Street, London, SE1 1GZ, telephone: 020 7939 000, fax: 020 7939 0001, www.cre.gov.uk.

The Equal Opportunities Commission, Arndale House, Arndale Centre, Manchester, M4 3EQ, telephone: 0845 601 5901, fax: 0161 838 8312, www.eoc.org.uk.

The Disability Rights Commission, DRC Helpline, Freepost MID02164, Stratford upon Avon, CV37 9BR, telephone: 08457 622 633, fax: 08457 778 878, www.drc.org.uk.

The Equality Commission for Northern Ireland, Equality House, 7–9 Shaftesbury Square, Belfast, BT2 7DP, telephone: 028 90 500600, www.equalityni.org.

Sexual harassment

Sexual harassment can take different forms. This includes:

- ✔ Indecent remarks.

- ✔ Comments about the way you look that make you feel uncomfortable or humiliated.

- ✔ Comments or questions about your sex life.

- ✔ Inappropriate touching or sexual demands.

- ✔ Bullying behaviour or being treated in a way that is rude, hostile, degrading, or humiliating because of your sex.

Men and women can be victims of sexual harassment at work. If this happens to you, tell a friend, colleague, or trade union representative, and ask the person harassing you to stop. It is a good idea to keep a written record of what happened, the days and times when it happened, and who else may have seen or heard the harassment. If the problem continues, report the person to your employer or trade union. Employers are responsible for the behaviour of their employees while they are at work. They should treat complaints of sexual harassment very seriously and take effective action to deal with the problem. If you are not satisfied with your employer's response, you can ask for advice and support from the Equal Opportunities Commission, your trade union, or the Citizen's Advice Bureau.

At Work

Both employers and employees have legal responsibilities at work. Employers have to pay employees for the work that they do, treat them fairly, and take responsible care for their health and safety. Employees should do their work with reasonable skill and care, and follow all reasonable instructions. They should not damage their employer's business.

A written contract or statement

Within two months of starting a new job, your employer should give you a written contract or statement with all the details and conditions for your work. This should include your responsibilities, pay, working hours, holidays, sick pay, and pension. It should also include the period of notice that both you and your employer must give for the employment to end. The contract or written statement is an important document and is very useful if there is ever a disagreement about your work, pay, or conditions.

Pay, hours, and holidays

Your pay is agreed between you and your employer. There is a minimum wage in the UK that is a legal right for every employed person above compulsory school leaving age. The compulsory school leaving age is 16, but the time in the school year when 16-year-olds can leave school in England and Wales is different from that in Scotland and Northern Ireland.

There are different minimum wage rates for different age groups. From October 2006 the rates are as follows:

- For workers aged 22 and above: £5.35 an hour.
- For 18–21-year-olds: £4.45 an hour.
- For 16–17-year-olds: £3.30 an hour.

Employers who pay their workers less than this are breaking the law. You can get more information from the Central Office of Information Directgov Web site, www.direct. gov.uk, which has a wide range of public service information. Alternatively, you can telephone the National Minimum Wage Helpline, telephone: 0845 600 0678.

Your contract or statement shows the number of hours you are expected to work. Your employer might ask you if you can work more hours than this and it is your decision whether or not you do. Your employer cannot require you to work more hours than the hours agreed on your contract.

If you need to be absent from work, for example if you are ill or you have a medical appointment, it is important to tell your employer as soon as you can in advance. Most employees who are 16 or over are entitled to at least four weeks, paid holiday every year. This includes time for national holidays. Your employer must give you a pay slip, or a similar written statement, each time you are paid. This must show exactly how much money has been taken off for tax and national insurance contributions.

Tax

For most people, tax is automatically taken from their earnings by the employer and paid directly to HM Revenue and Customs, the government department responsible for collecting taxes. If you are self-employed, you need to pay your own tax. Money raised from income tax pays for government services such as roads, education, police, and the armed forces. Occasionally HM Revenue and Customs sends out tax return forms, which ask for full financial details. If you receive one, it is important to complete it and return the form as soon as possible. You can get help and advice from the HM Revenue and Customs self-assessment helpline, telephone: 0845 300 45 45.

National Insurance

Almost everybody in the UK who is in paid work, including self-employed people, must pay National Insurance (NI) contributions. Money raised from NI contributions is used to pay contributory benefits such as the State Retirement Pension and helps fund the National Health Service. Employees have their NI contributions deducted from their pay by their employer every week or month. People who are self-employed need to pay NI contributions themselves: Class 2 contributions, either by direct debit or every three months and Class 4 contributions on the profits from their trade or business. Class 4 contributions are paid alongside their income tax. Anyone who does not pay enough NI contributions is not able to receive certain benefits, such as Jobseeker's Allowance or Maternity Pay, and may not receive a full state retirement pension.

Getting a National Insurance number

Just before their 16th birthday, all young people in the UK are sent a National Insurance number. This is a unique number for each person and it tracks their National Insurance contributions.

Refugees whose asylum applications have been successful have the same rights to work as any other UK citizen and to receive a National Insurance number. People who have applied for asylum and have not received a positive decision do not usually have permission to work and so do not get a National Insurance number.

You need a National Insurance number when you start work. If you do not have a National Insurance number, you can apply for one through Jobcentre Plus, or your local Social Security Office. It is a good idea to make an appointment by telephone and ask which documents you need to take with you. You usually need to show your birth certificate, passport, and Home Office documents allowing you to stay in the country. If you need information about registering for a National Insurance number, you can telephone the National Insurance Registrations Helpline on 0845 91 57006 or 0845 91 55670.

Pensions

Everyone in the UK who has paid enough National Insurance contributions receives a State Pension when they retire. The State Pension age for men is currently 65 years of age and for women it is 60, but the State Pension age for women is due to increase to 65 in stages between 2010 and 2020. You can find full details of the State Pension scheme on the State Pension Web site, www.thepensionservice.gov.uk or you can phone the Pension Service Helpline: 0845 60 60 265.

In addition to a State Pension, many people also receive a pension through their work and some also pay into a personal pension plan too. It is very important to get good advice about pensions. The Pensions Advisory Service gives free and confidential advice on occupational and personal pensions. Their helpline telephone number is 0845 601 2923 and their Web site address is www.opas.org.uk. Independent financial advisers can also give advice but you usually have to pay a fee for this service. You can find local financial advisers in the Yellow Pages and Thomson local guides, or on the Internet at www.unbiased.co.uk.

Health and safety

Employers have a legal duty to make sure the workplace is safe. Employees also have a legal duty to follow safety regulations and to work safely, and responsibly. If you are worried about health and safety at your workplace, talk to your supervisor, manager, or trade union representative. You need to follow the right procedures and your employer must not dismiss you or treat you unfairly for raising a concern.

Trade unions

Trade unions are organisations that aim to improve the pay and working conditions of their members. They also give their members advice and support on problems at work. You can choose whether to join a trade union or not and your employer cannot dismiss you or treat you unfairly for being a union member.

You can find details of trade unions in the UK, the bene-fits they offer to members, and useful information on rights at work on the Trades Union Congress (TUC) Web site, www.tuc.org.uk.

Problems at work

If you have problems of any kind at work, speak to your supervisor, manager, trade union representative, or some-one else with responsibility, as soon as possible. If you need to take any action, it is a good idea to get advice first. If you are a member of a trade union, your represen-tative can help you. You can also contact your local Citizen's Advice Bureau (CAB) or Law Centre. The national Advisory, Conciliation and Arbitration Service (ACAS) Web site, www.acas.org.uk gives information on your rights at work. ACAS also offers a national helpline, telephone: 08457 47 47 47.

Losing your job and unfair dismissal

An employee can be dismissed immediately for serious misconduct at work. Anyone who cannot do their job properly, or is unacceptably late or absent from work, should be given a warning by their employer. If their work, punctuality, or attendance does not improve, the employer can give them notice to leave their job.

It is against the law for employers to dismiss someone from work unfairly. If this happens to you, or life at work is made so difficult that you feel you have to leave, you may be able to get compensation if you take your case to an Employment Tribunal. This is a court that specialises in employment matters. You normally only have three months in which to make a complaint.

If you are dismissed from your job, it is important to get advice on your case as soon as possible. You can ask for advice and information on your legal rights and the best action to take, from your trade union representative, a solicitor, a Law Centre, or the Citizen's Advice Bureau.

Redundancy

If you lose your job because the company you work for no longer needs someone to do your job, or cannot afford to employ you, you may be entitled to redundancy pay. The amount of money you receive depends on the length of time you have been employed. Again, your trade union representative, a solicitor, a Law Centre, or the Citizen's Advice Bureau can advise you.

Unemployment

Most people who become unemployed can claim Jobseeker's Allowance (JSA). This is currently available for men aged 18–65 and women aged 18–60 who are capable of working, available for work, and trying to find work. Unemployed 16- and 17-year-olds may not be eligible for Jobseeker's Allowance but may be able to claim a Young Person's Bridging Allowance (YPBA) instead. The local Jobcentre Plus can help with claims. You can get further information from the Citizen's Advice Bureau and the Jobcentre Plus Web site: www.jobcentreplus.gov.uk.

New Deal

New Deal is a government programme that aims to give unemployed people the help and support they need to get into work. Young people who have been unemployed for 6 months, and adults who have been unemployed for 18 months, are usually required to join New Deal if they wish to continue receiving benefit. There are different New Deal schemes for different age groups. You can find out more about New Deal, telephone: 0845 606 2626 or: www.newdeal.gov.uk.

The government also runs work-based learning programmes that offer training to people while they are at work. People receive a wage or an allowance, and can attend college for one day a week to get a new qualification.

You can find out more about the different government schemes, and the schemes in your area, from Jobcentre Plus, www.jobcentreplus.gov.uk, or your local Citizen's Advice Bureau.

Working for Yourself

Tax

Self-employed people are responsible for paying their own tax and National Insurance. They have to keep detailed records of what they earn and spend on the business, and send their business accounts to HM Revenue and Customs every year. Most self-employed people use an accountant to make sure they pay the correct tax and claim all the possible tax allowances.

As soon as you become self-employed you should register yourself for tax and National Insurance by ringing the HM Revenue and Customs telephone helpline for people who are self-employed, on0845 915 4515.

Help and advice

Banks can give information and advice on setting up your own business and offer start-up loans, which need to be repaid with interest. Government grants and other financial support may be available. You can get details of these and advice on becoming self-employed from Business Link, a government-funded project for people starting or running a business – www.businesslink.gov.uk telephone: 0845 600 9 006.

Working in Europe

British citizens can work in any country that is a member of the European Economic Area (EEA). In general, they have the same employment rights as a citizen of that country or state.

Childcare and Children at Work

New mothers and fathers

Women who are expecting a baby have a legal right to time off work for antenatal care. They are also entitled to at least 26 weeks' maternity leave. These rights apply to full-time and part-time workers, and it makes no difference how long the woman has worked for her employer. It is, however, important to follow the correct procedures and to give the employer enough notice about taking maternity leave. Some women may also be entitled to maternity pay but this depends on how long they have been working for their employer.

Fathers who have worked for their employer for at least 26 weeks are entitled to paternity leave, which provides up to two weeks' time off from work, with pay, when the child is born. It is important to tell your employer well in advance.

You can get advice and more information on maternity and paternity matters from the personnel officer at work, your trade union representative, your local Citizen's Advice Bureau, the Citizen's Advice Bureau Web site – www.adviceguide.org.uk, or the government Web site www.direct.gov.uk.

Childcare

It is Government policy to help people with childcare responsibilities to take up work. Some employers can help with this. The ChildcareLink Web site www.childcarelink.gov.uk gives information about different types of childcare and registered child minders in your area, or telephone: 08000 96 02 96.

Hours and time for children at work

In the UK there are strict laws to protect children from exploitation and to make sure that work does not get in the way of their education. The earliest legal age for children to do paid work is 14. There are a few exceptions that allow children under the age of 14 to work legally and these include specific work in performing, modelling, sport, and agriculture. In order to do any of this work, it is necessary to get a licence from the local authority.

By law, children aged 14 to 16 can only do light work. There are particular jobs they are not allowed to do and these include delivering milk, selling alcohol, cigarettes, or medicines, working in a kitchen or a chip shop, working with dangerous machinery, or doing any other kind of work that might cause them any kind of injury. Children who work have to get an employment card from their local authority and a medical certificate of fitness for work.

The law sets out clear limits for the working hours and times for 14–16-year-old children. Every child must have at least two consecutive weeks a year during the school holidays when they do not work. They cannot work:

- ✔ For more than 4 hours without a one-hour rest break
- ✔ For more than 2 hours on any school day or a Sunday
- ✔ Before 7.a.m. or after 7.p.m
- ✔ For more than one hour before school starts
- ✔ For more than 12 hours in any school week

15- and 16-year-olds can work slightly more hours than 14-year-olds on a weekday when they are not at school, on Saturdays, and in school holidays. The local authority has a duty to check that the law is obeyed. If it believes that a young person is working illegally, it can order that the young person is no longer employed. You can find more information on the TUC Web site, www.worksmart. org.uk.

Part III
Questions and Answers

'The high ceilings, the wooden beams, the leaded windows – English houses are absolutely <u>steeped</u> in history.'

In this part...

*P*art III consists of over 300 multiple-choice
    questions that are representative of the types
of questions you're asked in the Life in the UK test.
I also include the answers so you can test yourself
until you're confident you can pass the exam
with ease.

Chapter 9

Sample Questions and Answers for the Life in the UK Test

· ·

*T*his chapter gives you an accurate example of the types of questions that crop up in the Life in the UK test. These aren't the exact questions that appear in your test, but they do cover similar information.

These questions are based on the information covered in Chapter 8, which comes from the Home Office's *Life in the United Kingdom* book.

Chapter 4 covers the ins and outs of taking, and retaking, the test. In the Life in the UK test, you must get around 18 of the 24 questions correct to pass the test and become a British citizen.

You can find the answers to these multiple-choice questions at the end of this chapter – but no cheating, now!

Good luck with your test!

Questions Based on Chapter 2

1. Why do migrants come to the UK?

    a) To claim benefits

    b) To escape persecution in their own country

    c) To find safety and in search of jobs and a better life

    d) To embark on a course of study

2. Why did the Protestant Huguenots come from France to the UK in the 16th and 17th centuries?

    a) To join the UK in a war with France

    b) For the excellence of local cuisine

    c) To find jobs

    d) To escape religious persecution

3. What caused the influx of Irish migrants in the 1840s?

    a) In response to the potato famine

    b) The industrial revolution meant there were many jobs in the UK

    c) As a staging post on their way to the United States

    d) Because Ireland was in civil war

4. From which three countries did Jewish people come to the UK to escape violence they faced at home between 1890–1910?

    a) France, Italy, and Germany

    b) Poland, Ukraine, and Belarus

c) Russia, Sweden, and Finland

d) Syria, Lebanon, and Jordan

5. In the 1980s the largest immigrant groups came from which countries?

a) Poland, Czech Republic, Hungary, Lithuania, and Estonia

b) Caribbean, Bangladesh, India, and South Asia

c) United States, Australia, South Africa, New Zealand Hong Kong, Singapore, and Malaysia

d) Spain, Italy, France, Portugal, Greece, Malta, and Cyprus

6. In the 1950s centres were set up in the West Indies to recruit workers for which occupations and industries?

a) Bus crews, textile, and engineering

b) Agriculture, fishing, and rubbish disposal

c) Legal profession, media, and education

d) Healthcare, civil service, and publishing

7. Since 1994 there has been a rise in the numbers moving to Britain from which parts of the world?

a) United states, western Europe, and Australasia

b) Latin and central America

c) Scandinavia and Nordic countries

d) Europe, the Middle East, Asia, Africa, and Indian Sub-Continent

8. **Recently the UK has introduced tighter immigration controls. Why?**

   a) To prevent terrorists from entering the UK

   b) To prevent unauthorised immigration and examine the claims of those seeking asylum more closely

   c) To properly verify that those coming to the UK can support themselves and won't prove a burden on the state

   d) To stop the smuggling of alcohol and tobacco products into the UK

9. **In the late 19th and early 20th century many UK women demonstrated for what right?**

   a) The right to vote

   b) The right to an abortion

   c) Equal pay and fairer treatment at work

   d) The right to be able to serve in the military

10. **When did British women first get the right to vote?**

    a) 1908

    b) 1918

    c) 1928

    d) 1938

11. **In what year was the voting age for women equalised with that** of men?

    a) 1908

    b) 1918

c) 1928

d) 1938

12. **In what year did married woman gain the right to divorce?**

a) 1857

b) 1887

c) 1907

d) 1037

13. **What percentage of the UK population are women?**

a) 49%

b) 50%

c) 51%

d) 52%

14. **What percentage of the UK workforce are women?**

a) 45%

b) 50%

c) 55%

d) 60%

15. **What proportion of women with children of school age are in paid work?**

a) One quarter

b) Half

c) Threequarters

d) All of them

16. By what percentage is the average hourly pay rate of women lower than men's?

    a) 5%

    b) 10%

    c) 15%

    d) 20%

17. How many young people, up to the age of 19, are there in the UK?

    a) 5 million

    b) 15 million

    c) 25 million

    d) 35 million

18. What proportion of children live with both birth parents?

    a) 85%

    b) 75%

    c) 65%

    d) 55%

19. In English and Scottish schools, children are given compulsory tests at which ages?

    a) 5,7, and 9

    b) 7, 11, and 14

    c) 12, 14, and 16

    d) 14, 16, and 18

20. **At age 16 most young people take GCSEs. What does GCSE stand for?**

    a) General Certificate of Secondary Erudition

    b) Great Certificate of Secondary Education

    c) Great Certificate of Secondary Erudition

    d) General Certificate of Secondary Education

21. **At age 17 and 18 many young people in the UK take what type of qualification?**

    a) A/S and A levels as well as vocational qualifications

    b) Driving test examination

    c) Bronze swimming certificate

    d) International baccalaureate

22. **What proportion of young people move onto higher education?**

    a) About one in ten

    b) About one in five

    c) About a third

    d) About a half

23. **How many children work in the UK?**

    a) None, it against the law

    b) About a million

    c) About two million

    d) About five million

24. What are the most common jobs young people do?

    a) Mining and textile work

    b) Newspaper delivery and work in super-markets and newsagents

    c) Advertising and media

    d) Healthcare and the legal profession

25. What is the minimum age for buying alcohol?

    a) There is no minimum age

    b) 16

    c) 18

    d) 21

26. What is the minimum age for buying tobacco?

    a) There is no minimum age

    b) 16

    c) 18

    d) 21

27. Amongst young people, do girls smoke more than boys, or boys more than girls?

    a) Girls smoke more than boys

    b) Boys smoke more than girls

    c) Smoking is banned in the UK

    d) Girls aren't allowed to smoke but boys are

28. **What proportion of young adults have used illegal drugs at least once?**

    a) Around a quarter

    b) Around half

    c) Around three quarters

    d) Nearly all

29. **What is the minimum voting age in the UK?**

    a) There is no minimum voting age

    b) 16

    c) 17

    d) 18

30. **What proportion of potential first-time voters actually cast their vote in the 2001 general election?**

    a) 8 out of 10

    b) 5 out of 10

    c) 4 out of ten

    d) 2 out of 10

31. **Name the main reason given by researchers why so few potential first-time voters actually cast their vote.**

    a) Polling stations aren't open late enough

    b) Distrust of politicians and the political process

    c) Not aware that election was taking place

    d) Everything is fine so why bother voting

32. **Name the five key political issues that young people in the UK say they're most concerned by.**

    a) Jobs, healthcare, education, taxation, and defence

    b) Foreign policy, environment, pensions, jobs, and education

    c) Crime, drugs, war/terrorism, racism, and health

    d) Defence, crime, healthcare, taxation, and pensions

33. **What percentage of young people have taken part in a community activity over the past year?**

    a) 6%

    b) 36%

    c) 56%

    d) 86%

34. **What proportion of young people have collected for charity or taken part in a fund-raising event in the past year?**

    a) A quarter

    b) A third

    c) Half

    d) Three quarters

35. **During the 1970s, the British Government admitted into Britain approximately how many people of Indian origin who were forced to leave Uganda because of persecution?**

a) None

b) 8,000

c) 28,000

d) 208,000

36. **When did the Soviet Union break up and people begin to come to Britain from Eastern Europe to seek a better life?**

a) Late 1990s to early 2000s

 b) Late 1980s to early 1990s

c) Late 1970s to early 1980s

d) Late 1960s to early 1970s

37. **In what year did married women gain the right to hold onto their own earnings and property?**

 a) 1882

b) 1902

c) 1922

d) 1942

38. **In which two decades did British society see increasing pressure from women for equal rights, and laws were passed entitling them to equal pay with men?**

 a) 1990s and 2000s

b) 1980s and 1990s

c) 1970s and 1980s

d) 1960s and 1970s

39. In which year did the First World War end?

a) 1908

b) 1918

c) 1928

d) 1938

40. What did women do in large numbers during the First World War?

a) Stay at home and look after the house

b) Fight and die on the Western Front

c) Demonstrate against the war and call for peace talks

d) Took on a much greater variety of work than they had done before, to help the war effort

41. What proportion of children live with both birth parents?

a) 5%

b) 35%

c) 65%

d) 75%

Questions Based on Chapter 3

42. What was the total population of the UK in 2005?

a) 60.8 million

b) 59.8 million

c) 56.8 million

d) 54.8 million

43. What was the population of England in 2005?

a) 30.4 million

b) 41.6 million

c) 45.5 million

d) 50.1 million

44. What was the population of Scotland in 2005?

a) 5.1 million

b) 6.5 million

c) 7.2 million

d) 12 million

45. What was the population of Wales in 2005?

a) 1.7 million

b) 2.3 million

c) 2.9 million

d) 5.2 million

46. What was the population of Northern Ireland in 2005?

a) 1.1 million

b) 1.7 million

c) 2.6 million

d) 3.8 million

47. The UK population has grown by what percentage since 1971?

    a) 7.7%

    b) 17.7%

    c) 27.7%

    d) 37.7%

48. Is it true or false that there are now more aged 60 and over than children under 16?

    a) True

    b) False

    c) They are equal

    d) There are no figures for different age groups

49. Name two parts of the UK that have seen their populations fall over the last 20 years.

    a) London and South-east

    b) South-west England and Wales

    c) The Midlands and London

    d) The North-west and North-east of England

50. In what year was the first census of the UK population carried out?

    a) 1801

    b) 1851

    c) 1901

    d) 1951

51. The next UK census is due in which year?

    a) 2008

    b) 2009

    c) 2010

    d) 2011

52. How often is the census carried out?

    a) Every year

    b) Every five years

    c) Every ten years

    d) Every twenty years

53. When do census records become available to be consulted freely?

    a) Immediately

    b) 10 years after the census is conducted

    c) 100 years after the census is conducted

    d) You're not allowed to consult the census records

54. What is the largest ethnic minority in the UK?

    a) People from Eastern Europe

    b) People of Caribbean descent

    c) People of Indian descent

    d) People from the United States

55. **What proportion of the African Caribbean, Pakistani, Indian, and Bangladeshi communities were born in the UK?**

    a) About half

    b) About a third

    c) About a quarter

    d) About one tenth

56. **Ethnic minorities make up what percentage of the UK population?**

    a) 5.6%

    b) 8.3%

    c) 9.1%

    d) 13.5%

57. **Ethnic minorities make up what percentage of the English population?**

    a) 5%

    b) 8%

    c) 9%

    d) 12%

58. **Ethnic minorities make up what percentage of the Welsh and Scottish population?**

    a) 2%

    b) 4%

    c) 6%

    d) 8%

59. **Ethnic minorities make up what percentage of the Northern Ireland population?**

   a) Less than 1%

   b) 3%

   c) 5%

   d) 7%

60. **What percentage of ethnic minorities live in London?**

   a) 10%

   b) 23%

   c) 37%

   d) 45%

61. **What percentage of London's residents are from ethnic minorities?**

   a) 6%

   b) 21%

   c) 29%

   d) 42%

62. **In the 2001 census, what percentage stated that their religion was Christian?**

   a) Around 90%

   b) Around 70%

   c) Around 60%

   d) Around 50%

63. **After Christianity what are the two next most common religions in the UK?**

    a) Muslim and Hindu

    b) Jedi and Voodoo

    c) Buddhist and Shinto

    d) Jewish and Sikh

64. **Is church attendance more common in Scotland, Wales, or England?**

    a) Scotland

    b) Wales

    c) England

    d) All about the same

65. **In which century did the Church of England come into existence?**

    a) Eleventh

    b) Sixteenth

    c) Nineteenth

    d) Twentieth

66. **Who holds the title 'supreme governor' of the Church of England?**

    a) The Prime Minister

    b) The Archbishop of Canterbury

    c) The Pope

    d) The monarch

67. Who is head of the Church of England?

    a) The Prime Minister

    b) The Archbishop of Canterbury

    c) The Pope

    d) The monarch

68. What percentage of the UK population is Catholic?

    a) About 10%

    b) About 20%

    c) About 30%

    d) About 40%

69. What is the distance from the north coast of Scotland to the south coast of England?

    a) Approximately 400 miles

    b) Approximately 600 miles

    c) Approximately 800 miles

    d) Approximately 1,000 miles

70. The Eid-IL-Fitr festival relates to which religion?

    a) Jewish

    b) Christian

    c) Hindu

    d) Muslim

71. **Apart from English, which two dialects are spoken in Northern Ireland?**

    a) Irish Gaelic and Ulster Scots

    b) Norwegian and Swedish

    c) Welsh and Scots Gaelic

    d) Irish Gaelic and Welsh

72. **The Scottish Gaelic language is spoken in which parts of Scotland?**

    a) Glasgow and Edinburgh

    b) Lowlands and Border region

    c) West coast and the Isle of Mull

    d) Highlands and Islands

73. **In which year was the Assembly for Wales created?**

    a) 1999

    b) 2001

    c) 2003

    d) 2005

74. **In which year was the Scottish Parliament created?**

    a) 1997

    b) 1999

    c) 2001

    d) 2003

75. Does England have its own parliament?

  a) There is no parliament based in England

  b) Yes, it's the House of Parliament in Westminster

  c) No, but it does host the UK Parliament in Westminster

  d) Yes, and it also hosts the UK Parliament in Westminster

76. Regional accents are common in the UK. Name the well-known dialect for people from London.

  a) Cockney

  b) Scouse

  c) Geordie

  d) Brummie

77. Name a well-known dialect for people from Liverpool.

  a) Scouse

  b) Cockney

  c) Geordie

  d) Brummie

78. Name a well-known dialect for people from Tyneside.

  a) Cockney

  b) Scouse

  c) Geordie

  d) Brummie

79. **Apart from London, which other parts of England have a large ethnic minority population?**

   a) Norfolk and Suffolk

   b) West Midlands and Yorkshire

   c) Cumbria and North-east

   d) South-west and East Midlands

80. **Which one of these four isn't a major UK sporting event?**

   a) Grand National

   b) Football Association Cup Final

   c) Breeders Cup

   d) Wimbledon tennis championship

81. **Name three sports played in Britain that enjoy a large, regular spectator following.**

   a) Football, cricket, and rugby

   b) Handball, lacrosse, and rowing

   c) Sumo, gridiron, and baseball

   d) Triathlon, downhill skiing, and bobsleigh

82. **Name the patron saint of Wales.**

   a) St Patrick

   b) St David

   c) St Andrew

   d) St George

83. **On what date is the national day of Wales celebrated?**

    a) 30th November

    b) 23rd April

    c) 17th March

    d) 1st March

84. **Name the patron saint of Northern Ireland and Ireland.**

    a) St Patrick

    b) St David

    c) St Andrew

    d) St George

85. **On what date is the national day of Northern Ireland and Ireland?**

    a) 30th November

    b) 23rd April

    c) 17th March

    d) 1st March

86. **Name the patron saint of England.**

    a) St Patrick

    b) St David

    c) St Andrew

    d) St George

87. On what date is the national day of England?

   a) 30th November

   b) 23rd April

   c) 17th March

   d) 1st March

88. Name the patron saint of Scotland.

   a) St Patrick

   b) St David

   c) St Andrew

   d) St George

89. What day is the national day of Scotland?

   a) 30th November

   b) 23rd April

   c) 17th March

   d) 1st March

90. What is the Notting Hill carnival?

   a) An international film festival

   b) A festival of art, music, and culture

   c) A giant trade fair

   d) A gay pride event

91. What date is Christmas Day?

   a) 5th November

   b) 1st April

      c) 26th December

      d) 25th December

92. What does Christmas Day celebrate?

      a) The birth of Jesus Christ

      b) The death and resurrection of Jesus Christ

      c) The end of the year

      d) Sales starting in the shops

93. The meat of what bird is traditionally eaten on Christmas Day?

      a) Turkey

      b) Chicken

      c) Ostrich

      d) Penguin

94. What date is Christmas Eve?

      a) 1 April

      b) 26 December

      c) 24 December

      d) 1 January

95. What Christmas folklore character is depicted dressed in red with a white beard?

      a) Father Christmas

      b) Mr Scrooge

      c) Robin red breast

      d) Mrs Christmas

96. What do British families usually do on Christmas day?

a) Hold a big party and invite the neighbours around

b) Fast and have a day of prayer

c) Set off fireworks and light a bonfire

d) Spend the day at home and eat a special meal

97. What date is Boxing Day?

a) 24th December

b) 26th December

c) 31st December

d) 1st January

98. What traditionally do Britons do on Boxing Day?

a) Stay at home and read

b) Go to work – it's a normal day

c) Visit family and friends and continue with the Christmas festivities

d) Light a bonfire and set off fireworks

99. When is New Year's Day celebrated in the UK?

a) 24th December

b) 26th December

c) 31st December

d) 1st January

100. What does Easter celebrate?

a) The crucifixion and subsequent resurrection of Jesus Christ

b) The entry of Jesus Christ into Jerusalem seven days prior to the crucifixion

c) The birth of Jesus Christ

d) The start of the summer

101. The Diwali festival relates to which UK minority religion?

a) Christianity

b) Hindu

c) Muslim

d) Jedi

102. When is Mothers' day?

a) Three weeks after Easter

b) Three weeks before Easter

c) Three weeks before Christmas

d) Three weeks after Christmas

103. When is St Valentine's Day?

a) 5th November

b) 31st December

c) 1st January

d) 14th February

104. Traditionally, what happens on St Valentine's Day?

   a) Bonfires are lit and fireworks set off

   b) A son cooks a special meal for his mother

   c) Lovers and husbands and wives generally exchange cards and gifts as a token of their love for one another.

   d) Everyone has a day off work

105. What happens on Mothering Sunday?

   a) Children, both young and old, give their mother chocolates, flowers, and try to make their day a nice one.

   b) Everyone has a day off

   c) Mothers have to prepare a special meal for their children and invite them around for festivities

   d) Husbands have to prepare a meal for their wives and the wives in turn must finish the meal in its entirety

106. On which date does April Fool's Day fall?

   a) 30th April

   b) 20th April

   c) 10th April

   d) 1st April

107. What do people do on April Fool's day?

   a) Exchange greetings cards and presents

   b) Invite family and friends around for food and drink

c) Play practical jokes on each other. (Sometimes even newspapers and television stations try to fool their readers and viewers with a phoney story.)

d) Dress up and go trick or treating

108. When is Guy Fawkes Night?

a) 5th November

b) 31st December

c) 1st January

d) 14th February

109. What is celebrated on Guy Fawkes night?

a) New Year

b) The birth of Jesus Christ

c) The foiling of a plot in 1605 to blow up the then King of England and the Houses of Parliament

d) The feast of St Guy Fawkes

110. Remembrance Day falls on 11th November each year. What is commemorated on this day?

a) Those people from the UK that died in the Second World War

b) Victims of the Bubonic Plague that hit the UK and Western Europe in the mid-14th century

c) The people who died in both World Wars and later conflicts

d) The Norman Conquest of Britain in 1066

111. **In what year did the First World War end?**

     a) 1914

     b) 1918

     c) 1939

     d) 1945

112. **What do many Britons now do on Remembrance Day?**

     a) Light bonfires and set off fireworks

     b) Put on fancy dress outfits and go trick or treating

     c) Host a meal for family and friends

     d) Hold a two-minute silence

Questions Based on Chapter 4

113. **General elections are held in Britain at least every how many** years?

     a) Five

     b) Four

     c) Six

     d) Three

114. **What does MP stand for?**

     a) Minister for Police

     b) Master of Parliament

     c) Member of Parliament

     d) Minister of Parliament

115. Who forms the Government?

a) Military commanders

b) The appointees of the Queen

c) Senior politicians from all the main political parties

d) MPs who belong to the largest political party in the House of Commons

116. There are two Houses of Parliament. One is the House of Commons, the other is called?

a) House of Cards

b) House of Lords

c) House of Wax

d) House of Westminster

117. The PM is the leader of the political party in power, what does PM stand for?

a) Powerful Man

b) Prime Minister

c) Powerful Minister

d) Political Manipulator

118. The PM lives at which famous address?

a) 11 Downing Street

b) Buckingham Palace

c) Westminster Abbey

d) 10 Downing Street

119. Who does the PM appoint and dismiss?

    a) The Queen or King's servants

    b) The Queen or King

    c) Ministers of State

    d) MPs

120. Who sits in the Cabinet?

    a) Ministers of State

    b) The PM's political advisers

    c) MPs

    d) Civil servants

121. Who is normally appointed a life peer?

    a) Ex-prime Ministers

    b) Church leaders

    c) Distinguished politicians, business people or lawyers

    d) People who make financial gifts to the government

122. How many people sit in the Cabinet?

    a) About 20

    b) 2 (that's all the people that can be fitted in)

    c) 10

    d) 40

123. How often does the Cabinet meet?

    a) Every day

    b) Once a week

    c) Once a fortnight

    d) Once a year

124. Which minister is responsible for the UK economy?

    a) The Governor of the Bank of England

    b) The PM

    c) The First Secretary to the Treasury

    d) The Chancellor of the Exchequer

125. Which minister is responsible for immigration and law and order?

    a) The PM

    b) The Chancellor of the Exchequer

    c) The Home Secretary

    d) The Foreign Secretary

126. Decisions made in Cabinet are submitted where for approval?

    a) The Queen

    b) The Houses of Parliament

    c) The electorate

    d) To a television vote

127. What type of constitution does the UK have?

    a) A written Bill of Rights

    b) A very ancient one

    c) An unwritten one

    d) It doesn't have a constitution

128. Where are new laws passed?

    a) In Cabinet

    b) In the Courts

    c) By the Queen

    d) In the Houses of Parliament

129. In the UK, the job of the Courts is to do what?

    a) Interpret laws passed in the Houses of Parliament

    b) Pass laws

    c) Sentence criminals

    d) Overrule politicians

130. Name the three main political parties in the UK.

    a) Republicans, Democrats, and Independents

    b) Nationalists, Republicans, and Liberals

    c) Conservative, Labour, and the Liberal Democrats

    d) Conservatives, Liberals, and Nationalists

131. The second largest party in the House of Commons is officially called?

    a) The losers

    b) The nearly men

    c) The Opposition

    d) Her Majesty's loyal Opposition

132. What is the Shadow Cabinet?

    a) Senior members of the second biggest party in parliament who shadow government ministers in different government departments

    b) Senior members of the biggest party in parliament who aren't quite important enough to sit in the real cabinet

    c) Very senior members of the full Cabinet who are asked to remain behind after meeting to discuss policy with the PM

    d) A meeting of the Cabinet which takes place at night

133. When are by-elections held?

    a) Half-way through the life of a parliament

    b) Every two years

    c) When an MP dies or resigns

    d) Whenever the government wants

134. Who opens parliament?

   a) The PM

   b) The reigning monarch

   c) A well-known celebrity

   d) The Chancellor of the Exchequer

135. In which year did the Prime Minister gain the power to appoint peers just for their lifetime?

   a) 1938

   b) 1958

   c) 1978

   d) 1998

136. What is the official title of the written record of proceedings in the Houses of Parliament called?

   a) Hanson

   b) Hansard

   c) The Sun

   d) Today in Parliament

137. Why is the UK said to have a 'free press'?

   a) There's no charge for newspapers or television

   b) You're free to say anything you want in the media

   c) It's free from government interference

   d) It's free of any original thoughts

138. **In practice what does the legal requirement for reporting of politics to be 'balanced' actually mean?**

    a) Giving equal time to rival viewpoints

    b) Asking tough questions of all politicians

    c) Giving free airtime to all political parties

    d) Allowing politicians to say what they want without questions

139. **What is the nickname for non-departmental public bodies?**

    a) The NHS

    b) The Civil Service

    c) NGOs

    d) Quangos

140. **The powers of the monarch are limited by what?**

    a) The army

    b) The powers of the monarch are unlimited

    c) The PM

    d) Constitutional law and convention

141. **In the UK, what must the reigning monarch always do?**

    a) Follow the advice of the PM on matters of government

    b) Give television interviews when asked

    c) Live in Buckingham Palace at weekends

    d) Attend parliament when asked

142. **Queen Elizabeth the Second has reigned since which year?**

   a) 1952

   b) 1977

   c) 2002

   d) 1932

143. **The official title of the heir to the throne is?**

   a) The Prince of Tides

   b) The Prince of Wales

   c) The artist formerly known as Prince

   d) The Prince of Britain

144. **When is the Queen's Speech made?**

   a) At Christmas on television

   b) At the beginning of a new session of parliament

   c) At the opening ceremony of the Commonwealth Games

   d) To the PM during her weekly audience

145. **What can the House of Lords do when presented with new laws from the House of Commons?**

   a) Throw them out and make new laws in its own right

   b) Tell the PM and the Queen what to do

    c) Sack MPs

    d) Delay the passage of the new laws but not overturn it

146. How many parliamentary constituencies are there throughout the UK?

    a) 100

    b) 650

    c) 645

    d) 745

147. What is the job of parliamentary committees?

    a) To spend hours debating political issues

    b) To scrutinise legislation and investigate administration

    c) To question ministers and the PM

    d) To draw up new law

148. How can you get to see parliamentary debates?

    a) On big screens in Trafalgar square

    b) You're not allowed to attend parliamentary debates

    c) By taking a seat in the public galleries through tickets or queuing at the public entrance

    d) Download a video podcast from iTunes

149. Who appoints or elects the Speaker of the House of Commons?

   a) Directly elected by the public

   b) Appointed by the Queen on the advice of the PM

   c) Elected through a ballot of members of the biggest political party in the Commons

   d) Elected through a ballot of all MPs

150. What is the job of the Whips in parliament?

   a) To ensure that all MPs are sober and behave properly

   b) To prevent members of the public from entering the Commons chamber

   c) To gather gossip for their party leaders

   d) Appointed by party leaders, to ensure discipline and attendance of MPs at votes in the House of Commons

151. What recently happened to the role of hereditary peers in the House of Lords?

   a) They were all sacked

   b) They had their automatic right to attend the House of Lords removed

   c) They were barred from ever coming to the House of Lords again

   d) They had their number expanded and some were given prominent government jobs

152. Who appoints Life Peers?

a) The PM

b) The Queen

c) They are self-appointed

d) The electorate gets to choose who should be a life peer

153. What does the 'first past the post' electoral system mean in practice?

a) The candidate with the majority of votes is elected

b) If there is no one candidate with a majority of vote the election is re-run

c) Whichever party polls the most votes throughout the country has all their candidates elected

d) The candidate with the most votes is elected

154. What does a political party need to form a government?

a) To have polled the largest number of votes at a general election

b) To have gained a majority of seats in the House of Commons

c) To have gained a majority of seats in the House of Commons and the House of lords

d) The approval of the Queen

155. The country house of the Prime Minister is called?

   a) Buckingham Palace

   b) Blenheim Palace

   c) Downing Street

   d) Chequers

156. What is the system used for elections to the Scottish Parliament, Welsh, and Northern Ireland Assemblies?

   a) First past the post

   b) Whichever party polls the most votes wins the election

   c) Proportional representation

   d) The public votes for their favourite party but not individual candidates

157. How many representatives from the UK are there in the European Parliament?

   a) 78

   b) 88

   c) 98

   d) 108

158. What tends to happen at Party Conferences?

   a) Party members get to vote on who should represent the party at election time

   b) The policy of the party is debated by the membership

     c) The leader of the party stands for re-election

     d) New members are welcomed to the party

159. What is a pressure group?

     a) MPs who are not aligned to a political party

     b) A commercial, financial, industrial, trade, or professional organisation

     c) A committee of MPs whose job it is to quiz leading civil servants to check they're doing a good job

     d) An organisation that tries to influence government policy directly or indirectly

160. What happens if the judiciary declares that a law passed by parliament contravenes human rights?

     a) They are ignored – parliament has the final say on the law

     b) The ruling automatically goes to the appeal court for further clarification

     c) The judge is sacked by the government

     d) Parliament is asked to consider changing the law

161. Who appoints judges?

     a) The Queen

     b) The Prime Minister

     c) A panel of other judges

     d) The Lord Chancellor

162. Where are the headquarters of the London Metropolitan Police?

a) New Scotland Yard

b) 221B Baker Street, London

c) The Old Bailey, London

d) The Royal Courts of Justice

163. What does police 'operational independence' mean?

a) The government cannot instruct the police to arrest or proceed against any individual

b) Members of the police force are immune from prosecution in the courts

c) The police do not have to follow what they're told to do by the courts

d) The police can arrest and imprison who they wish, when they want, for as long as they want

164. What is the job of the civil service?

a) To cover up government errors

b) To ensure that government policy is carried out

c) To ensure that government policy is seen in a favourable light in the media

d) To remain independent of the government at all times

165. **What happens to members of the civil service if, at a general election, the party in power changes?**

    a) Top civil servants are replaced by members of the new ruling party

    b) The civil service stops work and waits to be told what to do next

    c) They serve the new government loyally, looking to enact its policies

    d) They pick and choose which of the new governments policies they wish to enact

166. **Large towns and cities in the UK tend to be administered by one of the following:**

    a) An elected mayor

    b) The civil service in Whitehall

    c) A parish council

    d) A single authority such as a borough, metropolitan district, or city council

167. **What percentage of money for local authority services comes from the council tax?**

    a) 10%

    b) 20%

    c) 30%

    d) 40%

168. **Where does most of the money for local government come from?**

    a) The national lottery

    b) Council tax

    c) Central government funds

    d) A local income tax

169. **In which month are elections for local government held each year?**

    a) March

    b) April

    c) May

    d) June

170. **Wales and Scotland enjoy devolved government. What political issues are these institutions not allowed to make law on?**

    a) Health, education, and housing

    b) Pensions, legal affairs, and sport

    c) Social security, the environment, and rural affairs

    d) Defence, foreign affairs, and taxation

171. **In which city is the National Assembly for Wales based?**

    a) Cardiff

    b) Swansea

    c) Wrexham

    d) London

172. **How many members of the National Assembly for Wales are there and how frequently are elections held?**

   a) 60 members, elections every five years

   b) 60 members, elections every four years

   c) 50 members, elections every five years

   d) 50 members, elections every four years

173. **In which city is the Scottish Parliament based?**

   a) Dundee

   b) Glasgow

   c) Edinburgh

   d) Aberdeen

174. **How many members of the Scottish Parliament are there?**

   a) 329

   b) 229

   c) 129

   d) 29

175. **How many members does the Northern Ireland Assembly have?**

   a) 8

   b) 18

   c) 88

   d) 108

176. **When is the British government allowed to suspend the Northern Ireland Assembly?**

    a) Anytime it likes

    b) If the political leaders can no longer work together

    c) Every four years

    d) Every five years

177. **In which year was the Council of Europe created?**

    a) 1949

    b) 1945

    c) 1973

    d) 1956

178. **In which year was the Treaty of Rome that set up the EEC – the forerunner of the EU?**

    a) 1945

    b) 1947

    c) 1953

    d) 1957

179. **In which year did Britain join the European Union?**

    a) 1945

    b) 1949

    c) 1956

    d) 1973

180. What is the main stated aim of the European Union?

   a) For member states to become a single market

   b) The creation of a United States of Europe

   c) To have a military machine more powerful than America

   d) To ensure that the Eurovision song contest is broadcast in each member state

181. What special rights do citizens of EU states have?

   a) Freedom from arrest while travelling in other member states

   b) The right to travel to any EU country as long as they have a valid passport

   c) The right to claim state benefits while living in other member states

   d) The right to citizenship of all EU member states

182. Where is the European Commission based?

   a) Paris

   b) Brussels

   c) Strasbourg

   d) Berlin

183. How frequently are elections to the European Parliament held?

  a) Every four years

  b) Every five years

  c) Every six years

  d) Every seven years

184. What powers does the European Parliament have?

  a) The power to order the arrest of any citizen in any EU member state

  b) The power to impose taxes on the people of the UK

  c) The power to propose new laws for consideration by the council of ministers

  d) The power to scrutinise and debate the proposals and expenditure of the European Commission

185. What is an EU Regulation?

  a) A proposal to member states that they should change their own law

  b) A law change that must be introduced by member states within a set time

  c) A specific rule that automatically has the force of law in all EU countries

  d) A law that applies to all member states and, if broken, can lead to arrest and imprisonment

186. How many states are there in the Commonwealth?

  a) 184

  b) 104

  c) 84

  d) 53

187. What are the key aims of the Commonwealth?

  a) To develop democracy, eradicate poverty, and promote good government

  b) To become a economic and military rival to the United States

  c) To develop health programmes and deliver aid to starving people

  d) To ensure that the political and economic interests of the UK are furthered

188. What are the key aims of the United Nations?

  a) To develop health programmes and deliver aid to starving people

  b) To develop democracy, eradicate poverty, and promote good government

  c) To promote free trade

  d) To prevent war and maintain international peace and security

189. How many members of the UN security council are there?

  a) 5

  b) 10

c) 15

d) 20

190. **In which year was the present voting age of 18 set?**

a) 1919

b) 1929

c) 1969

d) 1989

191. **In order to vote in an election you must:**

a) Be on the electoral register

b) Be of sound mind and good character

c) Own property

d) Hold a British passport

192. **What is the deadline for return of electoral register forms?**

a) 15th March

b) 15th May

c) 15th August

d) 15th October

193. **Where is the electoral register held?**

a) The House of Parliament

b) Westminster Abbey

c) Local electoral registration office or library

d) Local registry office

194. **Citizens of the EU, resident in the UK, have the right to vote in which of the following?**

   a) Elections to the EU Parliament but no other elections

   b) All elections except national parliamentary elections

   c) Local council elections only

   d) No elections, they have to return to their home country to vote

195. **Citizens of the UK, Commonwealth, and which other country can vote in all public elections?**

   a) United States

   b) France

   c) Ireland

   d) Spain

196. **What age do you have to be before you can stand for election to public office?**

   a) 18

   b) 21

   c) 30

   d) 40

197. **What percentage of the vote must a candidate receive at an election to receive their deposit back?**

   a) 5%

   b) 10%

   c) 15%

   d) 20%

198. Who is head of the Commonwealth?

    a) The Archbishop of Canterbury

    b) The Queen

    c) The Prime Minister

    d) The President of the United States

199. To become elected as a local council you must:

    a) Live in the area and be on the electoral register

    b) Be a member of the Freemasons

    c) Own property

    d) Also be a member of parliament

200. Where can you find details of your local MP?

    a) Local newspaper advert

    b) Teletext

    c) Phone book, yellow pages, and local library

    d) The UK Parliament Web site

201. When an MP holds a 'surgery' what are they doing?

    a) Performing dental work on patients to supplement their salary

    b) Speaking at a public meeting

    c) Going out and knocking on the door of the electorate

    d) Allowing constituents to call in person to their office to raise matters of concern

Questions Based on Chapter 5

202. What proportion of UK people live in homes they own?

   a) Two thirds

   b) Half

   c) A third

   d) A quarter

203. What is a mortgage?

   a) A loan to buy a car

   b) A loan from a bank or building society to buy a house

   c) A type of life insurance policy

   d) A special loan for Muslim people looking to buy a house

204. How long does a mortgage term usually last?

   a) 5 years

   b) 15 years

   c) 25 years

   d) 35 years

205. In England and Wales where do you normally go first to find a home to buy?

   a) The police station

   b) Your local newspaper office

   c) An estate agent

   d) A solicitor

206. In Scotland where do you normally go to first to find a home to buy?

a) The police station

b) Your local newspaper office

c) An estate agent

d) A solicitor

207. What does an estate agent do?

a) Represents the person selling a home

b) Represents people looking to buy a home

c) Buys houses and rent them out

d) Collects property sales tax for the government

208. What does a subject-to-contract offer mean?

a) The offer is binding on all parties from the moment it's made

b) The offer can be withdrawn if for any reason the purchase can't be completed

c) The purchaser has paid a deposit to secure exclusive rights to buying the property

d) The offer is initially accepted but the seller can take another better offer from elsewhere if it's made

209. What checks does a solicitor make for you if you instruct him to help you buy a property?

a) Check that the property is structurally sound

b) Check that you can afford to buy the property

c) Check to see if your neighbours are quiet and well behaved

d) Carry out a number of legal checks on the property, the seller, and the local area

210. What does a surveyor do?

a) Arrange a loan to help you buy property

b) Put your offer to the seller

c) Check that the property is structurally sound

d) Check that the seller actually owns the property

211. From which source can you *not* rent a property?

a) The local council

b) The UK government in Westminster

c) Local housing association

d) Private landlords

212. Which body is responsible for providing social housing in Northern Ireland?

a) The Northern Ireland Assembly

b) The Northern Ireland Housing Association

c) The Northern Ireland Housing Executive

d) The Northern Ireland Police Service

213. Who is entitled to apply for council housing?

a) Everyone

b) Lone parents

c) The mentally ill

d) The homeless

214. How are applicants for council housing assessed?

a) Through a points system

b) Through an interview

c) According to how long they have lived in the area

d) According to their need for accommodation

215. What is a housing association?

a) A profit-making network of private landlords

b) An association formed by residents to help curb crime

c) The governing body for all UK local council housing departments

d) A not-for-profit organisation providing houses for rent

216. What is a tenancy agreement?

a) A record of all your rental payments

b) An agreement to buy a property

c) A set of rules you must follow while renting a property

d) An agreement to rent a property with someone else

217. **When renting a property how much of a deposit are you likely to be asked for?**

    a) Equivalent of one week's rent

    b) Equivalent of one month's rent

    c) Equivalent of six months' rent

    d) Equivalent of one year's rent

218. **What can your landlord *not* do while you are renting a property from him?**

    a) Enter the property

    b) Redecorate

    c) Raise the rent without your agreement

    d) Put the property up for sale

219. **How long usually does a tenancy agreement last?**

    a) Two years

    b) One year

    c) Six months

    d) One month

220. **What happens if you end the tenancy agreement before its fixed time?**

    a) You have to pay rent until the end of the term

    b) You can walk away after paying a week's rent

    c) You lose your deposit

    d) You're liable to prosecution

221. **If you're homeless, which organisation is legally obliged to provide help and advice?**

    a) The police station

    b) The local housing association

    c) A letting agent

    d) Local authority

222. **Which organisation can help with the cost of moving home?**

    a) Citizen's Advice Bureau

    b) The local housing association

    c) The social fund run by the department for work and pensions

    d) The police

223. **What is the fee levied for the supply of water to your home?**

    a) Water rate

    b) Water charge

    c) Domestic rates

    d) Bathing duty

224. **What is the standard voltage of electricity supplied to UK homes?**

    a) 60

    b) 120

    c) 180

    d) 240

225. **Who should you contact to find out who supplies your gas or electricity?**

    a) The local council

    b) Transco

    c) Energywatch

    d) Citizen's Advice Bureau

226. **Which organisation can you ask for advice on switching telephone services?**

    a) The local council

    b) Transco

    c) Ofcom

    d) Citizen's Advice Bureau

227. **What is the emergency number of the police, ambulance and fire service?**

    a) 999

    b) 911

    c) 111

    d) 000

228. **What is the main advantage of paying bills by standing order or direct debit?**

    a) You don't forget about them, as payment is automatic

    b) You can budget more easily

    c) You get preferential service from your supplier

    d) You often get money off your bill

229. Who collects household waste?

a) Your landlord

b) The local council

c) The department of the environment

d) A private company that you pay for

230. How are local government services paid for?

a) Through income tax

b) By a combination of central government grants and council tax

c) Through council tax

d) From central government grants

231. What determines the level of council tax?

a) How much your house may fetch if sold

b) Your income

c) The size and value of the house

d) Your income and size of your house

232. What percentage discount do people who live on their own get off their council tax bill?

a) 75%

b) 50%

c) 35%

d) 25%

233. Which other groups can qualify for a discount from their council tax bill?

a) Disabled people

b) People from Scotland

c) People who work for the local council

d) People who live in rented accommodation

234. If you have problems with your neighbours what should you do first?

a) Speak to them and try to reason with them

b) Complain immediately to the local council

c) Call the police

d) Go to the courts and try to get an injunction

235. What does council tax pay for?

a) Repairs to your home

b) National defence

c) Education and healthcare

d) Local government services, refuse collection, and emergency services.

236. What bank note denominations are used throughout the UK?

a) £2, £4, £6, £8, and £10

b) £1, £5, £10, £100, and £1,000

c) £5, £10, £20, and £50

d) £1, £10, £100, and £1,000

237. **In which year was the euro adopted by 12 European states, but not by the UK?**

a) 2000

b) 2001

 c) 2002

d) 2003

238. **What documents may you need to produce in order to be allowed to open a current account?**

a) British citizenship test pass certificate

b) A copy of your pay slip

c) A passport or driving licence

d) A letter from your doctor or solicitor saying that you are of good character

239. **When do you use a personal identification number?**

a) When withdrawing money from a cash machine

b) When talking to your bank or building society

c) When talking with immigration authorities

d) When trying to open a bank or building society account

240. **How do store cards differ from credit cards?**

a) Money borrowed from a store card must be repaid within a month

b) Borrowing is always more expensive on store cards than credit cards

c) The amount of money you can borrow on store cards is always less than on a credit card

d) Store cards can only be used in an individual shop or group of shops

241. What happens if you do not pay off all the money borrowed on a store card when sent a monthly bill?

a) You have to pay non-payment penalties

b) You're charged interest on the outstanding balance

c) You're taken to court by the card provider

d) If you own a home, it's taken from you

242. What is a credit union?

a) A trade union that represents bank workers

b) The body representing all UK lenders

c) A local council organisation that gives out loans

d) A financial cooperative, controlled by its members

243. Who cannot claim state benefits?

a) Disabled people

b) People who have no legal rights to UK residency

c) The unemployed

d) People who have a job

244. In which year did the National Health Service start in the UK?

- a) 1908
- b) 1928
- c) 1948
- d) 1968

245. What does GP stand for?

- a) General Practitioner
- b) General Physician
- c) Great Physician
- d) Great Practitioner

246. How do you get to see an NHS specialist?

- a) Go to hospital and ask to see one
- b) Call an ambulance
- c) Go to your GP surgery and ask to see one
- d) Go to your GP who may refer you to one

247. Where should you go in the case of a medical emergency?

- a) Nearest hospital accident and emergency department (A&E)
- b) Your local GP surgery
- c) The local council
- d) The nearest hospital of whatever sort

248. **GP treatment is free but you can be asked to pay for what?**

   a) An ambulance in an emergency

   b) Medicines and some vaccinations

   c) X-rays

   d) Missed appointments with your GP

249. **What are you entitled to when registering with a GP?**

   a) Money-off vouchers at your local chemists

   b) A free X-ray

   c) A free health check

   d) A free consultation with the GP

250. **Who does *not* pay for sight tests in England and Wales?**

   a) Local government employees

   b) NHS employees

   c) People over the age of 50

   d) People over the age of 60

251. **What is a health visitor?**

   a) A qualified nurse who advises you on caring for a baby

   b) A qualified nurse who advises you on how to stay healthy

   c) A social worker who checks on the condition of your children

   d) A doctor who visits your home when you're unwell

252. What does NHS Direct do?

    a) Arranges for a doctor to visit you

    b) Books appointments with your GP

    c) Arranges for an ambulance in an emergency

    d) Provides information about health services and medical conditions

253. How long do you have in which to register a baby with the Registrar of Births, Marriages, and Deaths?

    a) 6 days

    b) 6 weeks

    c) 6 months

    d) 16 months

254. If the parents of the baby are unmarried, who is the only person allowed to register the birth?

    a) The mother

    b) The father

    c) The GP

    d) A solicitor

255. In the UK (excluding Northern Ireland) between what ages is it compulsory for all children to attend school?

    a) Between ages 3 and 16

    b) Between ages 5 and 18

    c) Between ages 5 and 16

    d) Between ages 3 and 18

256. **At what age do children in the UK (excluding Scotland) attend secondary school?**

    a) 11

    b) 13

    c) 9

    d) 15

257. **State education is free in the UK but parents are asked to pay for what?**

    a) The heating costs of the school

    b) The cost of examination

    c) The cost of uniforms and sports wear

    d) The cost of schoolbooks

258. **What are 'independent schools'?**

    a) Schools that are tied to a particular church, synagogue, or mosque

    b) Schools that select their pupils by examination

    c) Schools where the pupils also live during term time

    d) Schools that are not paid for by the state

259. **What percentage of UK children attend independent schools?**

    a) 6%

    b) 8%

    c) 10%

    d) 12%

260. Which subject is not in the national curriculum?

   a) Religious education

   b) History

   c) Geography

   d) Maths

261. In England at what ages are the four key stage tests taken?

   a) 5, 7, 9, and 11

   b) 7, 9, 11, and 13

   c) 7, 11, 13, and 15

   d) 7, 11, 14, and 16

262. What is the name of the government's national service for young people offering career advice?

   a) Connexions

   b) Connected

   c) Careers plus

   d) Career advice service

263. How many days per a year must UK schools be open?

   a) 160

   b) 190

   c) 220

   d) 250

264. **At what age are UK children allowed to leave school, or stay and take their A levels?**

   a) 21

   b) 18

   c) 16

   d) 14

265. **What is the name of the package of financial help available to the children of low-income households?**

   a) Education maintenance allowance

   b) Student grants scheme

   c) Student loan company

   d) Education support scheme

266. **What is the chief difference between the university education system in England and Wales and Scotland?**

   a) University students in England and Wales automatically receive more money in the form of student loans

   b) University courses in Scotland always last a year longer than they do in England and Wales

   c) In Scotland there are no up-front tuition fees to pay

   d) Students applying for courses in Scotland have to have better A levels then their counterparts from England and Wales

267. **What dues the film classification 'U' stand for?**

    a) Universal

    b) Unclassified

    c) Unfunny

    d) Unwatchable

268. **At what age are British citizens entitled to a free TV licence?**

    a) 75

    b) 70

    c) 65

    d) 60

269. **What is the name of the UK charity set up to look after important buildings and parts of the countryside?**

    a) Barnados

    b) National Treasure

    c) National Heritage

    d) National Trust

270. **At what age are people in the UK allowed to be served alcohol in pubs?**

    a) 21

    b) 18

    c) 17

    d) 16

271. **From what age are you allowed to drive a large bus or lorry in the UK?**

   a) 21

   b) 18

   c) 17

   d) 16

272. **The UK driving test comes in two parts; what are those two parts?**

   a) A physical examination and a practical driving test

   b) A practical driving test and a full eye examination

   c) A written theory test and a practical driving test

   d) A written theory test and a physical examination

273. **What is the speed limit on UK motorways?**

   a) 100 mph

   b) 70 mph

   c) 55mph

   d) There is no speed limit on motorways

Questions Based on Chapter 6

274. Which government department supplies guidance on who is allowed to work in the UK?

    a) The Department for Work and Pensions

    b) The Department of the Environment

    c) The Home Office

    d) The Foreign and Commonwealth Office

275. Where can you find job adverts?

    a) In national, local newspapers, and job centres

    b) In the Yellow pages

    c) In telephone boxes

    d) On street billboards

276. What help is available at Job Centre Plus branches?

    a) They dress you for interviews

    b) They advise you on finding work and claiming benefits

    c) They find you a government job

    d) They tell you what to say at interviews

277. If you have qualifications from abroad, which agency can help you see how they compare with UK qualifications?

    a) The Home Office

    b) National Academic Recognition Information Centre

c) Department for Education and Skills

d) The passport and identity service

278. What is a job covering letter?

a) A letter you attach to a CV or application form

b) A letter outlining what skills you have that relate to the job

c) A letter setting out that you accept an offer of work

d) An introductory letter from the Job Centre to be handed over at interview

279. What do referees do?

a) They decide whether or not you should get the job

b) They vouch that you do not have a criminal record

c) They vouch that you have the legal right to work in the UK

d) They supply a reference outlining why you're suitable for the job

280. What can happen to people who tell lies at a job interview?

a) They can go to prison

b) They can be deported

c) Nothing

d) They can be sacked

281. Where can you find out more about English language training?

a) Job Centre Plus

b) The local library, Web sites and colleges

c) The Home Office

d) The Foreign office

282. Which of these grounds is it unlawful to discriminate against a worker?

a) Height

b) Weight

c) Sexual orientation

d) Personal hygiene

283. Men and women doing the same job should receive what?

a) The same size of desk

b) The same pay

c) The same promotion prospects regardless of ability

d) The same free lunches

284. Which body can help with discrimination issues?

a) Commission for racial quality

b) The Home Office

c) The police

d) Commission for Equality and Human Rights

285. **If you're being sexually harassed, what is it a good idea to do?**

   a) Keep a written record of all sexual harassment incidents

   b) Leave the job immediately

   c) Denounce the harasser in public

   d) Report it to the police

286. **How long is it before an employee is legally obliged to supply you with a written contract of employment?**

   a) By the end of the second day of employment

   b) By the end of the second month of employment

   c) By the end of the second year of employment

   d) Employers are not legally obliged to give you a contract

287. **How many days are you entitled to take off work each year?**

   a) 5

   b) 10

   c) 20

   d) 30

288. What information must your pay slip show?

    a) How many hours you have worked

    b) Your holiday entitlement

    c) Your job title

    d) How much has been deducted from your pay in tax and national insurance

289. Which organisation is responsible for sending you a self-assessment tax return?

    a) Job Centre Plus

    b) HM Treasury

    c) HM Revenue and Customs

    d) Social security office

290. Just before which birthday are all UK people sent a national insurance number?

    a) 16

    b) 18

    c) 21

    d) 30

291. Where can you obtain a national insurance number?

    a) The Post Office

    b) Job Centre Plus or social security office

    c) The Border and Immigration Agency

    d) HM Revenue & Customs

292. **What is the state pension age for men?**

    a) 55

    b) 60

    c) 65

    d) 70

293. **What is the current state pension age for women?**

    a) 55

    b) 60

    c) 65

    d) 70

294. **Where can you get free advice on pension matters?**

    a) Your bank

    b) Job Centre Plus

    c) The Border and Immigration Agency

    d) Pensions Advisory service

295. **Who is legally responsible for health and safety in the workplace?**

    a) The employer

    b) The employee

    c) The government

    d) The police

296. When should you consider going to employment tribunal?

    a) When trying to get a pay rise

    b) When needing advice about whether you're being harassed at work

    c) If you're sacked unfairly or you've left work after unfair treatment

    d) When you want to get a better job

297. When could you be entitled to redundancy pay?

    a) When you take time off work sick

    b) When you're sacked for misconduct

    c) When you work overtime

    d) When you're dismissed because your employer no longer needs someone for your job

298. What is the name of the benefit available for unemployed people?

    a) Job seeker's allowance

    b) Dole money

    c) Tax credits

    d) Disability living allowance

299. What does the New Deal do?

    a) Gives money to unemployed people

    b) Helps people from abroad learn English

    c) Pays a state pension

    d) Offers help and support to get unemployed people back to work

300. What does Business Link do?

a) Helps match up employers with workers

b) Provides information and advice for business

c) Provides business loans

d) Is a market for small business to sell their wares

301. How long does a new father have to have worked for his employer before being entitled to paternity leave?

a) 6 weeks

b) 6 months

c) 6 years

d) 16 years

302. How long are women allowed to take off work for maternity leave?

a) 2 weeks

b) 26 weeks

c) 1 year

d) 18 months

303. What is the earliest legal age at which children can do most jobs in Britain?

a) 10

b) 12

c) 14

d) 16

304. Which of these jobs is a child legally not allowed to do?

    a) Sell alcohol

    b) Sell cars

    c) Sell newspapers

    d) Stacking shelves

Answers

● ●

Here are the answers to those questions. Check below to see how you did.

Answers to the Questions Based on Chapter 2

1. c

2. d

3. a

4. b

5. c

6. a

7. b

8. b

9. a

10. b

11. c

12. a

13. c

14. a

15. c

16. d

17. b

18. c

19. b

20. d

21. a

22. c

23. c

24. b

25. c

26. b

27. a

28. b

29. d

30. d

31. b

32. c

33. d

34. c

35. c

36. b

37. a

38. d

39. b

40. d

41. c

Answers to the Questions Based on Chapter 3

42. b

43. d

44. a

45. c

46. b

47. a

48. a

49. d

50. a

51. d

52. c

53. c

54. c

55. a

56. b

57. c

58. a

59. a

60. d

61. c

62. b

63. a

64. a

65. b

66. d

67. d

68. a

69. b

70. d

71. a

72. d

73. a

74. b

75. c

76. a

77. a

78. c

79. b

80. c

81. a

82. b

83. d

84. a

85. c

86. d

87. b

88. c

89. a

90. b

91. d

92. a

93. a

94. c

95. a

96. d

97. b

98. c

99. d

100. a

101. b

102. b

103. d

104. c

105. a

106. d

107. c

108. a

109. c

110. c

111. b

112. d

Answers to the Questions Based on Chapter 4

113. a

114. c

115. d

116. b

117. b

118. d

119. c

120. a

121. c

122. a

123. b

124. d

125. c

126. b

127. c

128. d

129. a

130. c

131. d

132. a

133. c

134. b

135. b
136. b
137. c
138. a
139. d
140. d
141. a
142. a
143. b
144. b
145. d
146. c
147. b
148. c
149. d
150. d
151. b
152. a
153. d
154. b
155. d
156. c
157. a
158. b
159. d

160. d

161. d

162. a

163. a

164. b

165. c

166. d

167. b

168. c

169. c

170. d

171. a

172. b

173. c

174. c

175. d

176. b

177. a

178. d

179. d

180. a

181. b

182. b

183. b

184. d

185. c

186. d

187. a

188. d

189. c

190. c

191. a

192. d

193. c

194. b

195. c

196. b

197. a

198. b

199. a

200. c

201. d

Answers to the Questions Based on Chapter 5

202. a

203. b

204. c

205. c

206. d

207. a

208. b

209. d

210. c

211. b

212. c

213. a

214. a

215. d

216. c

217. b

218. c

219. c

220. a

221. d

222. c

223. a

224. d

225. b

226. c

227. a

228. d

229. b

230. b

231. c

232. d

233. a

234. a

235. d

236. c

237. c

238. c

239. a

240. d

241. b

242. d

243. b

244. c

245. a

246. d

247. a

248. b

249. c

250. d

251. a

252. d

253. b

254. a

255. c

256. a

257. c

258. d

259. b

260. a

261. d

262. a

263. b

264. c

265. a

266. c

267. a

268. a

269. d

270. b

271. a

272. c

273. b

Answers to the Questions Based on Chapter 6

274. c

275. a

276. b

277. b

278. a

279. d

280. d

281. b

282. c

283. b

284. d

285. a

286. b

287. c

288. d

289. c

290. a

291. b

292. c

293. b

294. d

295. a

296. c

297. d

298. a

299. d

300. b

301. b

302. b

303. c

304. a

Index

• *G* •

Notes

FOR DUMMIES

A Reference for the Rest of Us!

FOR DUMMIES®

A Reference for the Rest of Us!